Reset and Rise

A Guide to Building Habits That Stick

T.J. Lane

© **Copyright 2025 - All rights reserved.**

The content contained within this book may not be reproduced, duplicated or transmitted without direct written permission from the author or the publisher.

Under no circumstances will any blame or legal responsibility be held against the publisher, or author, for any damages, reparation, or monetary loss due to the information contained within this book, either directly or indirectly.

Legal Notice:

This book is copyright protected. It is only for personal use. You cannot amend, distribute, sell, use, quote or paraphrase any part, or the content within this book, without the consent of the author or publisher.

Disclaimer Notice:

Please note the information contained within this document is for educational and entertainment purposes only. All effort has been executed to present accurate, up to date, reliable, complete information. No warranties of any kind are declared or implied. Readers acknowledge that the author is not engaged in the rendering of legal, financial, medical or professional advice. The content within this book has been derived from various sources. Please consult a licensed professional before attempting any techniques outlined in this book.

By reading this document, the reader agrees that under no circumstances is the author responsible for any losses, direct or indirect, that are incurred as a result of the use of the information contained within this document, including, but not limited to, errors, omissions, or inaccuracies.

Table of Contents

INTRODUCTION 1

CHAPTER 1: THE ART OF THE RESET 5
- DEFINING A RESET 6
  - *Types of Resets* 7
  - *Identifying When You Need a Fresh Start* 9
- THE BENEFITS OF A RESET 10
  - *Gives You Clarity* 10
  - *Allows You to Explore New Possibilities* 11
  - *Offers a Chance to Reflect* 11
  - *Offer Deeper Insight* 12
  - *Starting Small: The Key to Sustainable Reset* 12
- BUILDING A RESET MINDSET 13
  - *Key Elements of a Reset Mindset* 14
- EMBRACING THE POWER OF RESET: A PATH TO LASTING GROWTH AND SUCCESS 16

CHAPTER 2: RISE WITH INTENTION 17
- INTENTIONAL GOALS VERSUS TREND-FOLLOWING 18
  - *Identifying Your Core Values* 20
- PERSONALIZED, MEANINGFUL GOAL SETTING 20
  - *Spend Time Reflecting* 21
  - *Align Goals With Your Strengths and Passions* 21
  - *Use the SMART Framework* 21
  - *Consider Your Current Life Circumstances* 22
  - *Harness the Power of Technology* 22
  - *Create a Vision Board or Journal* 23
- ALIGNING INTENTIONS WITH ACTIONS 24
  - *Be Clear About Your Intentions* 24
  - *Practice Self-Assessment* 25
  - *Employ Habit Staking* 26
- EMBRACING INTENTIONAL HABITS: YOUR PATH TO AUTHENTIC GROWTH 27

CHAPTER 3: BUILDING THE HABIT LOOP 29
- UNDERSTANDING TRIGGERS IN THE HABIT LOOP 31
  - *Contextual Triggers* 31
  - *Emotional Triggers* 32
  - *Time-Based Triggers* 32
  - *Social Triggers* 33
- STRUCTURING SUSTAINABLE ROUTINES 34

- Set Micro-Habits 34
- Use Habit Stacking 35
- Be Flexible in Your Approach 35
- REINFORCING HABITS WITH REWARDS 36
  - Personalized Rewards 37
  - Social Rewards 37
  - Gamification 38
  - Aligning Rewards to Personal Values 38
- WORKSHEET: IDENTIFYING PERSONAL TRIGGERS AND REWARDS TO REINFORCE NEW HABITS 39
- APPLYING THE HABIT LOOP 40

CHAPTER 4: START SMALL, AIM HIGH 41

- SCIENCE OF INCREMENTAL PROGRESS 42
  - The Benefits of Taking Incremental Steps 43
- BREAKING DOWN BIG TASKS 44
  - Time Block Your Day 45
  - Create a Checklist 45
  - Look at Past Achievements 47
- PRACTICAL EXAMPLES OF SCALING GOALS 48
  - The Fitness Journey 48
  - Learning a New Skill 48
  - The Professional Realm 49
  - Creative Pursuits 49
- EMBRACING SMALL BEGINNINGS 50

CHAPTER 5: NAVIGATING SETBACKS AND ROADBLOCKS 51

- RECOGNIZING PATTERNS IN SETBACKS 52
  - Identify Triggers 52
  - Identifying Loss of Motivation 52
  - Notice if You Self-Sabotage 53
  - Practice Self-Reflection 53
- EMBRACING INCREMENTAL PROGRESS 54
  - Embrace Setbacks as a Natural Part of the Process 55
  - Focus on Consistent Changes 55
  - Practice Self-Compassion 55
  - Set SMART Goals 56
- BOUNCING BACK FROM SETBACKS 57
  - Turning Setbacks Into Learning Opportunities 58
  - The Role of Self-Compassion 58
- EMBRACING GROWTH AND PROGRESS 59

CHAPTER 6: CREATING A SUPPORT SYSTEM 61

- THE POWER OF ACCOUNTABILITY PARTNERS 62

FINDING THE RIGHT MENTORS AND COMMUNITY GUIDANCE 64
   Find Someone Who Aligns With Your Goals 64
   Set Clear Expectations 64
   Join a Support Group 65
MAPPING PERSONALIZED SUPPORT SYSTEMS 66
WORKSHEET: MAPPING OUT YOUR PERSONAL SUPPORT SYSTEM 66
   Step 1: Identify Your Goal(s) 66
   Step 2: Reflect on Your Needs 67
   Step 3: Analyze Your Current Support System 68
   Step 4: Fill the Gaps 68
   Step 5: Visualize Your Support System 69
   Step 6: Set Clear Expectations 69
   Step 7: Track Your Progress and Celebrate Wins! 69
BUILDING A SUPPORT SYSTEM THAT LASTS 70

CHAPTER 7: SUSTAINABLE MOMENTUM 73

KEEPING HABITS FRESH AND ENGAGING 74
   Evaluate Your Routine 75
   Set Mini Goals 75
   Celebrate Your Achievements 75
   Use Visual Reminders 76
   Share Your Journey 76
STRATEGIES TO PREVENT BURNOUT 77
   Incorporate Downtimes 77
   Set Realistic Goals 78
   Cultivate a Positive Mindset 78
   Lean on Others For Support 79
   Let Go of Perfectionism 79
RE-EVALUATING YOUR HABITS 80
   Seek Feedback 80
   Be Adaptable 81
   Celebrate Your Wins 81
   Embrace Failure as Part of the Process 82
   Set Milestones 82
   Building Momentum: Turning Small Wins Into Lasting Progress 82

CHAPTER 8: THE RESET AND RISE HABIT PLAN 85

CRAFTING YOUR PERSONALIZED HABIT ROADMAP 86
   Goal-Setting Worksheet: Define and Celebrate Progress 87
   Implementing Your Plan 90
SETTING AND CELEBRATING MILESTONES 91
   Create a Balance Between Short-Term Wins and Long-Term Goals 92
   Celebrate Your Accomplishments 92
   Remain Adaptable 92

- TRACKING PROGRESS AND REFLECTING ON HABITS 94
  - *Practice Journaling* *94*
  - *Use Digital Apps* *94*
  - *Reflect Regularly* *95*
  - *Celebrate Success and Learn From Setbacks* *95*
  - *Harness the Power of Community* *96*
- BUILDING YOUR ROADMAP TO LASTING GROWTH 96

CHAPTER 9: ROUTINES THAT ELEVATE 99

- CREATING EMPOWERING ROUTINES 100
  - *Morning Routine* *100*
  - *Afternoon Routine* *101*
  - *Evening Routine* *102*
  - *Weekend Routine* *103*
- DESIGNING PERSONALIZED MORNING AND EVENING RITUALS 104
  - *Morning Rituals* *105*
  - *Evening Rituals* *105*
- WEEKLY PREPARATIONS FOR SUCCESS 106
  - *Weekly Review Sessions* *106*
  - *Time Blocking for Priorities* *107*
  - *Meal and Nutrition Plans* *107*
  - *Scheduling Self-Care Activities* *108*
- CHECKLIST: CREATING ROUTINES THAT ALIGN WITH YOUR PERSONAL AND PROFESSIONAL GOALS 108
- THE POWER OF INTENTIONAL ROUTINES 109

CONCLUSION 111

APPENDIX A 115

- HABIT FORMATION TEMPLATE 115
  - *Weekly Tracker* *115*
  - *Reflections* *116*
  - *Measuring Progress* *116*
- MONTHLY HABIT TRACKER 116

APPENDIX B 117

- HABIT LOOP BREAKDOWN 117
  - *Instructions* *117*
  - *Step 1: Identify the Habit* *117*
  - *Step 2: Define the Habit Loop* *117*
  - *Step 3: Reflect and Adjust the Habit Loop* *118*
  - *Step 4: Create a Habit Action Plan* *119*
- DAILY HABIT TRACKER 121
- STREAK TRACKER 122

APPENDIX C **123**

RESOURCE LIST FOR DEVELOPING NEW HABITS AND RESETTING YOUR LIFE 123
    Books *123*
    Apps *124*
    Podcasts.. *124*
ONLINE COURSES 125
OTHER RESOURCES 125
ONLINE COMMUNITIES 126

REFERENCES **127**

Introduction

Be willing to be a beginner every single morning. –Meister Eckhart

Imagine standing at the threshold of a new season, a time when nature itself invites renewal. The air feels charged with possibility—a promise of change and new beginnings. In the fast-paced whirlwind of modern life, where to-do lists stretch endlessly, and schedules leave little room to breathe, the idea of a fresh start holds undeniable appeal. But what gives these new beginnings their true power? It's not just about leaving the past behind; it's about seizing the opportunity to redefine your journey from the ground up.

For young professionals, balancing personal goals with demanding work schedules can feel like an uphill climb. There's always another deadline, another meeting, or another task demanding attention. Amid this professional whirlwind, the quiet desire to form healthier habits often gets buried, whispering faintly beneath the chaos. Yet that desire—

persistent and steady—remains a constant reminder of the meaningful changes you long to make.

Setbacks are an inevitable part of life. Unexpected changes can throw your world off balance, leaving you searching for direction. In these moments of uncertainty, a fresh start can act as a guiding light, offering clarity and structure to transform your routines into productive, life-giving habits. It's not just about starting over; it's about rebuilding stronger.

For parents and caregivers, the challenge often lies in juggling the demands of nurturing others while striving for personal growth. How do you set a positive example for your children while still making space for your own development? It can feel like walking a tightrope without a safety net. But fresh starts aren't just about individual growth; they can extend to your whole family, sparking positive change that benefits everyone.

The magic of a fresh start lies in its promise: a blend of hope and real potential for transformation. Yet, why does creating lasting habits often feel so elusive? Forming habits isn't just about willpower; it's about understanding and addressing the psychological and behavioral patterns that make them so difficult to maintain. Consider this: 80% of New Year's resolutions fail by mid-February (Bodell, 2022). This isn't due to a lack of determination, but to the hidden challenges we all face in building habits that stick.

What if true success isn't about sheer determination but about learning how to reset when things go off track? Imagine viewing setbacks not as failures but as opportunities to pause, reflect, and adjust. That's the heart of the Reset and Rise philosophy—turning small resets into lasting, transformative habits.

Through the *Reset and Rise* framework, you'll discover how every small choice can ignite meaningful change. Each reset offers a fresh beginning, and this book will guide you through the highs and lows of transformation, showing you how to grow stronger with every step forward.

Think about J.K. Rowling, who faced tremendous challenges before becoming the world-renowned author of *Harry Potter*. As a single mother living on welfare and struggling with depression, she could have allowed rejection from multiple publishers to end her dream. Instead, she treated each setback as a reset—a chance to improve her manuscript and try again. Her resilience transformed her vision into one of the most successful book series in history, inspiring millions.

Or consider Oprah Winfrey, who was fired from her first television job as an anchor in Baltimore and was deemed "unfit for television" (Ward, 2017). Rather than letting this rejection derail her aspirations, she viewed it as an opportunity to reset and pivot, eventually creating *The Oprah Winfrey Show* and becoming one of the most influential media personalities in the world.

Now, think about a time in your life when you faced a daunting challenge. Maybe it felt like standing at the base of a mountain, unsure if you could climb it. Yet, one small decision to reset helped you find a new way forward. This book is designed to bring you to those pivotal moments again and again, equipping you with the tools to unlock your potential for change.

Within these pages, you'll find practical advice, relatable stories, and encouragement to tackle everyday struggles. Purposeful habits aren't reserved for a lucky few; they're achievable for anyone willing to embrace the *Reset and Rise* journey. It's about crafting a life marked by growth, resilience, and meaningful change.

So, whether you're striving to balance the demands of work and life, recovering from life's curveballs, or setting an example for your children, remember that a fresh start is always within reach. All it takes is the courage to take that first step—to reset and rise.

Let this book be your guide. Together, we'll explore the power of resetting through actionable strategies and insights into the nature of habit formation. As you turn each page, you'll uncover your natural capacity for change and empowerment.

As we begin this journey, take a moment to imagine the life you want—one not limited by past failures or fears but strengthened by the lessons you've learned. Embrace the promise of a fresh start and greet each day with renewed energy. Whether you're a young professional navigating life's uncertainties or a parent modeling healthier habits, this is your moment to begin again.

Chapter 1:
The Art of The Reset

You must learn a new way to think before you can master a new way to be. —
Marianne Williamson

One rainy Monday morning, I sat at my desk, staring at a pile of unfinished work, the weight of anxiety pressing heavily on my chest. My inbox overflowed with unopened emails, each a reminder of missed deadlines and forgotten commitments. My mind raced with thoughts of all the tasks that had slipped through the cracks, and I felt as though I was drowning in a sea of obligations. With each tick of the clock, the pressure mounted. The rain tapping against the window mirrored the storm inside me—a turbulent mix of frustration, self-doubt, and exhaustion. My heart raced as I hovered over the mouse, unsure if I had the strength to face what awaited me.

Listening to the rain tapping on the window, I recalled my grandmother's wise words: "Sometimes, the best thing you can do is hit the reset button." Her words resonated deeply as I stood up, took a deep breath, and paused everything for a moment. I stretched, cleared my mind, and grabbed a notepad and pen. I wrote down three small tasks I could complete that day. That simple act of releasing self-criticism and starting fresh brought a sense of calm and renewed purpose. It was like pressing a reset button on my day.

We all face times when we feel stuck—whether in our jobs, personal lives, or our goals. At those moments, what we need more than anything is a fresh start!

While a reset can be rewarding, it can also be challenging because it demands courage and self-reflection. It requires you to let go of past mistakes and the comfort of familiar patterns, even when they no longer serve you. This process can be uncomfortable, as it involves facing difficult truths and stepping into the unknown. However, whether you're working on building better habits or trying to find a new direction, a reset is something we all need at some point in our lives.

If you're facing unexpected changes or feeling stuck after a setback, a reset can help you take control and move forward. It gives you the chance to pause, release the past, and focus on what truly matters, bringing hope and fresh energy to your life. However, it's important to remember that a reset isn't about forgetting the past—it's about learning from it and moving forward. In this chapter, I'll guide you through the process of resetting your habits and provide simple tools to help you turn setbacks into opportunities for growth and positive change.

Defining a Reset

Life is filled with unexpected twists and turns, and sometimes, our best-laid plans fall apart. Whether it's a missed workout, a failed diet plan, or an emotional setback, the feeling of starting over can seem daunting. But what if we saw these moments not as failures but as opportunities to start over? This is the essence of a reset—a chance to pause, reassess, and begin again, wiser and stronger than before.

When we think of a reset, it often brings to mind a fresh start—a new beginning. It might involve hitting the pause button, stepping away from the chaos, and reflecting on where you are versus where you want to be. However, a true reset is not just about changing your circumstances; it's about transforming your mindset, approach, and actions. Whether you're facing a major life shift, dealing with a personal setback, or simply feeling stuck, resetting your life means reassessing your goals, your values, and the habits that may no longer serve you. It might involve making tough decisions—cutting out unhealthy relationships, leaving behind old habits that are holding you back, or perhaps taking a leap into something new and unfamiliar. The idea of a reset can feel overwhelming at first, like stepping into the unknown, but it's also an exciting opportunity for growth and transformation. It's about finding the courage to let go of past mistakes or regrets and moving forward with the confidence that you can create something better for yourself.

Resetting your life might mean embracing a new routine, adopting a healthier lifestyle, or even changing your perspective on challenges. It's a process of realigning with your authentic self, prioritizing what really matters, and shedding the weight of things that no longer contribute to your happiness or success. In essence, a reset is about reclaiming control and setting a new course for the future—one where you are empowered to make choices that reflect your deepest aspirations and bring you closer to the life you desire.

Types of Resets

You can reset various areas of your life—your habits, emotions, or situations—and regain focus, clarity, and motivation. For example, when you've been struggling with a particular habit, a reset might involve taking a break, reassessing your approach, and then coming back with a renewed strategy. It's not about erasing past efforts, but rather learning from them and using those lessons to create better, more effective habits or responses in the future. In simple terms, a reset is like pressing the restart button on your mindset or actions, giving you a clean slate to work from and a chance to move forward with new energy and a fresh perspective.

There are different types of resets, each serving a unique purpose depending on the situation.

Emotional reset: When you're overwhelmed by feelings of frustration or disappointment, an emotional reset is crucial. For example, when you're overwhelmed by a disagreement with a close friend. Instead of reacting impulsively, you could take a step back and practice deep breathing or take a short walk to clear your mind. During this time, you focus on calming your emotions and gaining perspective. An emotional rest helps clear emotional clutter, enabling you to tackle challenges with a balanced and focused mindset. This process creates space for calm reflection, allowing you to respond rather than react.

Situational reset: Significant changes, such as starting a new job, moving to a new city, or navigating major life transitions, often require a situational reset. These moments call for adaptability. A situational reset allows you to pause, reassess your approach, and realign your strategies with the new circumstances. This process not only reduces stress but also fosters personal growth and informed decision-making.

Long-term reset: A long-term reset is essential when you've been feeling stuck for a while or need to change your habits completely. For example, when you realize you've been in the same job for years and feel stuck or unfulfilled. After taking time to reflect on your goals and what truly matters, you might decide to pursue a completely new direction, like going back to school for a different field or starting your own business. A long-term reset is a chance to reflect on what's working and what's not and make room for new ideas that better align with your evolving goals. Adjusting a long-term reset to fit your personal needs can be a powerful tool for lasting growth and change.

Resets help you develop a growth mindset by shifting your focus from fixed outcomes to new possibilities. This mindset encourages you to forgive yourself for setbacks and see them as valuable parts of the learning process. Instead of aiming for perfection, you start seeing progress as the real goal. Take Kate, for example; she felt overwhelmed by frustration after a series of conflicts with her family. Rather than letting those emotions spiral, she decided to take a weekend for herself to spend time introspecting and reflecting on her emotions. By giving herself this space, Kate returned to her family conversations with a calmer mindset, ready to listen and communicate more effectively. This emotional reset didn't erase the problems, but it gave her the clarity to handle them with more compassion and patience.

Forgiving past mistakes is key to growth. It builds resilience and reinforces the belief that no obstacle is insurmountable. When you see resets as opportunities for growth, you gain confidence in your ability to change. This mindset motivates you to step outside your comfort zone and take on new challenges.

Identifying When You Need a Fresh Start

It's important to recognize when you need a reset. Look out for signs of burnout, repeated failures, or a lack of motivation. These are often signals telling you it's time for a change. For instance, if you're starting a new job in a different city, the workload and unfamiliar environment can leave you feeling stressed and lost. Realizing when you need a situational reset can help you take a step back to reassess your current situation. It can help you find ways to move forward. You may need to create a new daily routine, reach out to your colleagues for support, and give yourself grace as you adjust. These actions can help you adapt to your new circumstances and rebuild your confidence.

So, how do you initiate a successful reset? Start by identifying which area of your life needs change—whether it's emotional, situational, or long-term. Reflect on what you've learned from past experiences and set realistic goals that align with your current priorities. Remember that meaningful change takes time and effort, so be patient and persistent. Small steps lead to bigger results over time. Each step forward brings you closer to a better version of yourself. We'll discuss in detail how taking small, manageable steps can help you achieve your bigger goals in Chapter 4.

The Benefits of a Reset

Resets can be a powerful way to shed the emotional burdens we carry. Imagine walking along a familiar path where each step feels heavier due to the weight of past failures and unmet goals. It's like running with weights strapped to your ankles. A reset is the moment you remove those weights, freeing yourself from emotional baggage and regaining momentum. When you choose to let go of what's holding you back, you make room for new energy and motivation. A reset allows you to refuel your spirit and move forward with a fresh sense of purpose.

Let's look at some of the benefits of taking time to reset.

Gives You Clarity

Hitting the reset button brings clarity. Think of your priorities as puzzle pieces scattered on a table. Over time, some pieces get lost or misplaced. A reset allows you to take a step back, reassess the bigger picture, and put those pieces back together in a way that makes sense. This clearer perspective helps you set goals that align with your long-term aspirations. When you know what really matters, you can focus your energy more effectively and take meaningful steps toward fulfillment.

Imagine you've been juggling work, family, and personal goals, feeling like you're constantly spinning plates. Over time, it's easy for your priorities to become unclear when you're trying to handle everything at once. Taking a step back for a reset, for instance, setting aside a quiet weekend for reflection—can help you see the bigger picture. You might realize that your health or relationships have taken a backseat while you prioritize work demands. By identifying what truly matters to you—your well-being—you can reorganize your schedule, set clearer boundaries, and focus on what aligns with your long-term goals. This reset can reduce stress and bring a balance to your life.

Allows You to Explore New Possibilities

There's something exciting about a fresh start. It's like standing at the edge of an unexplored landscape full of possibilities. This sense of novelty can be incredibly motivating. Just like an artist facing a blank canvas, you get to create something new and inspiring. Picture yourself setting up an easel in front of a vast, empty canvas—each stroke of the brush represents a new choice, decision, and opportunity to express your creativity. You might not yet know what the final image will look like, but the potential of what could be fills you with energy and curiosity.

Similarly, when you begin a new habit or set a new goal, you're charting an unknown territory. Think about deciding to adopt a healthier lifestyle. At the outset, your journey is like that blank canvas—unformed but brimming with promise. Each small decision you make, whether it's choosing a nutritious meal or taking a short walk, adds a brushstroke to your evolving picture. The promise of potential achievements fuels your enthusiasm, turning what might seem like minor efforts into meaningful progress. The excitement of imagining the end result—a healthier, more energized version of yourself—keeps you motivated to continue the journey step by step.

Offers a Chance to Reflect

Resets offer valuable moments for reflection. They give you a chance to look back at your journey with curiosity and openness instead of judgment. By examining what worked and what didn't, you can uncover important insights about your habits and decisions. These reflections help you create better strategies for the future, allowing you to avoid past mistakes and cultivate personal growth. The key is to ask the right questions and be honest with yourself about the answers. What might seem like a setback often holds lessons that can guide you forward with more wisdom and confidence.

Let's say you've been trying to establish a consistent workout routine, but keep falling off track. Instead of beating yourself up, take a moment to reflect. Ask yourself why it hasn't worked—maybe the timing doesn't fit your schedule, or the workouts feel too intense. By identifying the obstacles, you can adjust your plan, like choosing shorter workouts or finding a different time of day. This reset helps you move forward with a more realistic and effective approach, turning what seemed like failure into a building block for success.

Offer Deeper Insight

Resets offer deeper personal insight. In today's fast-paced world, it's easy to lose sight of yourself amid constant external pressures. Resetting allows you to reconnect with your core values and rediscover your inner compass. Spending time in reflection guides you toward more authentic decisions and actions. By cultivating this self-awareness, you can make choices that align with who you truly are, fostering a sense of purpose and fulfillment beyond surface-level accomplishments. For instance, if you've been saying yes to every opportunity at work, hoping to advance your career, but you feel drained and disconnected. During a reset, take a moment to reflect on what truly matters to you. You may realize that creativity and family time are core values you've neglected. With this insight, you might decide to set boundaries at work and dedicate time to a hobby you love or to family activities. This not only restores balance but also helps you live in a way that feels more meaningful and true to yourself.

Starting Small: The Key to Sustainable Reset

Reflection requires setting aside some quiet time without distractions. Think about key moments in your life—whether they were wins or challenges—and focus on your emotions and the choices you made during those times. Keeping a reflection journal can be helpful in this process. It allows you to record your thoughts and explore them honestly. When you look back at what you've written, you might notice patterns or progress that you hadn't noticed before.

If you're juggling a hectic schedule, learning to reset can be life-changing. With endless responsibilities, it's easy to fall into routines that seem productive but leave you feeling unfulfilled. Taking a reset gives you a chance to pause, reassess your priorities, and realign your efforts with your goals. This intentional recalibration helps you strike a healthier balance between work and leisure, boosting your overall well-being and job satisfaction. For example, if you find yourself working late every night, the constant stress can wear you down. A reset might involve stepping back and setting clear boundaries around your work hours. Making time for rest or hobbies can improve your personal life and help you regain focus and efficiency at work.

Similarly, if you're recovering from a setback or major life change, a reset can give you hope and direction. Transitioning to a new phase isn't just about leaving the past behind; and it's about learning from your experiences and using them to build a stronger foundation for the future. Think of a reset as a chance to turn a challenging chapter into an empowering story. Consciously choosing to reset gives you confidence and reinforces the belief that change is possible, no matter how difficult your circumstances may be.

If you're a parent or caregiver, mastering the art of resetting can also greatly impact your family. You're not just managing your own life, but setting an example for your children. By showing them how to approach obstacles with creativity and resilience, you teach them valuable life skills like flexibility and perseverance. For instance, if your family plan falls through, finding an alternative activity shows your kids how to adapt and stay optimistic when faced with challenges. These lessons will help them handle life's ups and downs confidently.

Building a Reset Mindset

Developing a reset mindset is key to building healthier habits. It encourages you to view setbacks as opportunities for growth rather than as failures. Embracing this perspective can turn challenges into invaluable learning experiences that support your ongoing journey toward building better habits.

When we face obstacles, it's easy to feel discouraged. However, if you view these setbacks as learning opportunities, you shift your focus from what went wrong to what you can improve. For example, if you're trying to exercise daily but miss a few days due to unexpected circumstances, instead of seeing this as a failure, take it as a chance to reassess your approach—perhaps you need to adjust to your schedule or identify triggers that disrupt your habit. Each setback becomes a building block for stronger and more resilient habits.

Key Elements of a Reset Mindset

Building a reset mindset involves shifting from a fixed mindset—changing your perspective from seeing failure as a dead end to a growth mindset—where every experience is a chance to learn and improve.

Let's look at some key elements for building this mindset.

Self-Compassion

Practicing self-compassion is a crucial element of a reset mindset. It's easy to be hard on yourself during challenging times, but being kind to yourself can help you build resilience and improve your mental well-being. When you face a setback, ask yourself: Would you speak to a friend the way you speak to yourself? Treating yourself with the same understanding and encouragement you'd offer a friend can ease feelings of guilt and open pathways to improvement.

To practice self-compassion, regularly check in with yourself. Set aside moments to reflect on your feelings, acknowledge your efforts, and remind yourself that stumbling is part of the learning process. This habit promotes a supportive inner dialogue and builds resilience in the long haul.

Adaptability

Resilience strengthened by adaptability is key to maintaining a reset mindset. Being flexible allows you to adjust your approach when needed, keeping you moving forward even when life throws unexpected challenges your way. Sometimes, things don't go exactly as planned, but having an open mind helps you pivot quickly, turning obstacles into opportunities for creativity and growth. For example, if work demands disrupt your new nutrition plan, don't abandon your goals—instead, adapt by preparing quick, healthy meals ahead of time. Being open to change means accepting the need to make adjustments without resisting them. It helps you view different situations and changes as natural parts of life.

Visualizing Your Outcomes

Visualization techniques are powerful post-reset tools. They help you picture your success clearly, boosting your confidence and motivation to stick with new habits. Envisioning a positive outcome reinforces the belief in your ability to achieve your goals.

To include visualization in your reset process, create a mental image of achieving your goals. If you're working toward a career goal, like earning a promotion, visualize yourself confidently leading a team meeting or receiving recognition for a successful project. Imagine the pride and satisfaction of reaching this milestone, feeling valued and accomplished. This mental image reinforces your motivation and helps you stay focused on the daily actions that will lead you to achieve your goal, such as improving your skills or taking on new challenges.

Incorporate Micro-Resets Into Your Routine

Incorporating micro-resets into your daily routine can make a huge difference in building new habits. These small, deliberate pauses help you check in with yourself and stay aligned with your goals. They keep minor challenges from turning into major setbacks, ensuring you stay on track.

For example, you could set a clear intention each morning or take short breaks during the day to assess your emotions. These simple steps help you reset quickly, keeping you focused on your bigger goals. Making micro-resets a regular part of your day can help you handle minor disruptions without losing momentum. Look for natural points in your day where these resets can fit in smoothly—maybe during your commute or between tasks at work. Use those moments to pause, breathe, and refocus.

A reset mindset requires cultivating resilience, practicing self-compassion, and using visualization techniques alongside micro-resets. These strategies form a holistic approach, turning setbacks into learning opportunities. Each challenge you face can offer valuable insights that guide you forward, leading to lasting success as you form healthier habits.

Embracing the Power of Reset: A Path to Lasting Growth and Success

Resets in habit formation offer much more than just a fresh start—they give you opportunities for deeper self-discovery and meaningful growth. Whether you need an emotional, situational, or long-term reset, these intentional pauses address various challenges in the journey of transformation. Whether you're juggling work commitments, navigating a major life transition, or you're a parent striving to be a positive role model to your kids, embracing resets can redefine your journey toward healthier habits.

Remember, the reset mindset isn't about perfection, but it's about progress. It encourages you to view setbacks as opportunities for growth rather than stumbling blocks. By practicing self-compassion, visualization techniques, and incorporating micro-resets into your daily routine, you'll turn obstacles into opportunities for reflection and growth.

Embracing a reset mindset helps you build resilience, stay open to change, adapt easily, and keep learning as you go. So, whether you're adjusting your daily routine or reimagining long-term goals, take time to reflect and reset because every fresh start is not only a beginning but a powerful tool supporting your path to lasting success.

Chapter 2:

Rise With Intention

The victory of success is half won when one gains the habit of setting goals and achieving them. –Og Mandino

Imagine waking up each morning not just going through the motions, but feeling deeply connected to your purpose. Instead of hitting snooze and dreading the day ahead, you open your eyes with a sense of excitement and direction. Each moment, from your first sip of coffee to your last task at work, transforms into a deliberate step toward a larger goal.

What if every choice you made, no matter how small, contributed to something meaningful? Picture starting your day with intention, knowing that your actions align with what you value most. Whether it's dedicating time to personal growth, nurturing relationships, or pursuing a passion project, each decision becomes an opportunity to create a life that reflects your authentic self. The ordinary turns into the extraordinary, not because the tasks themselves change, but because you approach them with clarity and purpose.

This mindset shifts your entire perspective, turning challenges into opportunities for growth and setbacks into valuable lessons. By living with intention, you're not just passing time—you're building a legacy, one intentional choice at a time.

Living with intention isn't just a passing trend—it's a transformative way to align your choices and habits with your true self. Intentional living invites you to pause and reflect, uncovering your deepest motivations and setting goals that align with your core values. Instead of being swayed by fleeting trends or external pressures, this approach focuses on building a meaningful connection to what truly matters in your life.

Contrasting temporary trends with the depth of intentional living reveals how to create habits that foster genuine growth and long-lasting change. With consistent, actionable steps, you can turn abstract aspirations into practical routines that not only enhance your well-being but also align with your life's greater purpose.

Intentional Goals Versus Trend-Following

In today's fast-paced world, it's easy to be drawn in by the latest trends that promise quick fixes or life-changing results. However, these surface-level approaches often lack the depth necessary for genuine personal growth. Following trends without reflection can distract you from what truly matters—building habits that align with your core values and intentions.

Intentional habits, on the other hand, are born from thoughtful self-reflection and a conscious commitment to what is genuinely important to you. When you explore your motivations, desires, and long-term goals, you can create routines that resonate deeply with your values rather than succumbing to external pressures. These value-driven habits are not only more sustainable but also more rewarding because they reflect who you are and what you truly care about.

Trends often set an unrealistic expectation, which can quickly lead to burnout. They promote behaviors that might not align with your natural strengths or interests, pushing you beyond your limits. Research shows that a lack of control over one's actions is a major factor contributing to burnout (Maslach and Leiter, 2016). In contrast, when your actions are rooted in personal autonomy and values, engagement and satisfaction increase—both in professional environments and everyday life. This principle underscores the importance of intentionality, and it empowers you to make choices that are not only more manageable but also deeply fulfilling.

Chasing after fleeting trends often leads to disappointment when the initial excitement fades, leaving behind unfulfilled promises and unsustainable habits. Trends are usually designed for mass appeal and are rarely tailored to individual needs or values. As a result, following them can leave you feeling disconnected from your true goals and identity—struggling to maintain practices that never aligned with your intentions in the first place.

On the other hand, prioritizing authenticity over conformity allows you to connect deeply with your goals and identity. When you base your habits on core values rather than popular fads, you create a foundation of resilience and purpose. There's a greater sense of empowerment that comes with knowing your choices reflect your authentic self, not just the current craze. This connection promotes emotional satisfaction and stability, creating an environment conducive to personal and professional success.

Consider the wave of extreme fad diets as a clear example. While these diets promised rapid weight loss, many people soon regained weight because the restrictive routines were impractical and unsustainable (Panoff, 2024). On the other hand, someone who intentionally adopts balanced nutrition based on their health goals is more likely to succeed long-term. Their habit stems from thoughtful reflection and personal commitment, reducing the risk of setbacks and dissatisfaction. This contrast illustrates the power of intentional living. When your actions align with genuine values, they become enduring sources of fulfillment and growth.

Identifying Your Core Values

Setting guidelines can help you cultivate personal values through intentional habit formation. Start by identifying your core values—those aspects of life that matter most to you—it could be family, creativity, health, or self-improvement. These values should guide your daily decisions and habits. For example, if personal growth is a key value for you, your actions may include setting aside time for self-reflection, journaling, or taking courses that align with your goals. This intentionality ensures that each choice you make, whether it's how you spend your time or what new habits you adopt, supports your larger life narrative, preventing conflict between daily actions and intrinsic motivations.

Equally important are the practical steps that turn your intentions into reality. Start by setting clear, manageable goals that reflect your values. For example, if health is your priority, set achievable milestones like preparing nutritious meals or incorporating daily walks. Small, consistent successes build momentum and reinforce your commitment. Visual reminders or affirmations can keep your values front and center, helping you stay focused. Additionally, practicing daily reflection or journaling allows you to review your progress, providing clarity and accountability.

Living a life driven by personal values rather than external trends empowers you to create meaningful, lasting change. When your habits align with your deepest intentions, each step becomes a building block toward greater fulfillment and purpose. This builds resilience against burnout and dissatisfaction, breaking the cycle of pursuing fleeting trends and guiding you toward what truly matters to you.

Personalized, Meaningful Goal Setting

No matter where you are in life—whether you're bouncing back from setbacks or managing the challenges of parenting while juggling countless responsibilities—setting meaningful goals can be life-changing.

Personalization is key to unlocking motivation and success. Tailoring your goals to your unique circumstances and aspirations makes them more engaging and attainable. This approach can significantly enhance your chances of achieving those goals.

Let's look at a few strategies to set personalized, meaningful goals.

Spend Time Reflecting

Setting meaningful goals begins with introspection. Reflecting on what truly matters to you helps distinguish genuine desires from societal and familial expectations. Often, we chase goals that don't align with our authentic selves simply because we've been conditioned to value them. Asking reflective questions can help uncover what you genuinely want. Questions like, "What am I passionate about?" or "What legacy do I want to leave?" guide you toward deeper understanding and alignment with your core values. By focusing on your intrinsic motivations rather than succumbing to external pressures, you set a pathway toward fulfillment and satisfaction.

Align Goals With Your Strengths and Passions

Next, align your goals with your strengths and passions. Think about what you're naturally good at and what you've been praised for in the past. Setting goals that leverage your strengths will increase motivation and make your progress feel more rewarding. Similarly, choose goals that ignite your enthusiasm. Whether it's a hobby you love or a cause you care about, pursuing something you're passionate about will keep you engaged and motivated.

Use the SMART Framework

To turn your reflections into actionable steps, the SMART framework can be quite useful. Using the SMART—Specific, Measurable, Achievable, Relevant, and Time-bound framework ensures that your goals are clear and structured. For instance, rather than vaguely deciding to be healthier, setting a specific target, like exercising three times a week for 30 minutes, creates a measurable and achievable objective. This clarity allows you to track your progress and refine your strategies, turning aspirations into tangible achievements.

Additionally, ensuring your goals are achievable can help you stay motivated. While ambitious goals can be motivating, setting unrealistic goals can lead to frustration and abandonment. Try aiming for incremental improvements to achieve a sense of accomplishment and stay inspired in the process.

Relevance is equally important in goal setting—goals must align with your personal values and life mission, creating a seamless connection between your day-to-day activities and long-term aspirations.

Setting deadlines for your goals adds a sense of urgency, promotes accountability and commitment, and encourages prompt action while minimizing procrastination. If you're balancing work and family responsibilities, this structured approach ensures that you allocate time and resources wisely, keeping your efforts aligned with your priorities. Using the SMART framework can turn goals into powerful tools for cultivating intentionality and a sense of purpose.

Consider Your Current Life Circumstances

It's also important to consider your current life circumstances. Be realistic about your time, energy, and commitments. If you're juggling work, family, and social obligations, choose goals that fit into your lifestyle without causing burnout. If you're in a season of life where things are particularly busy, adjust your goals to reflect that. For example, instead of committing to two-hour yoga sessions every day, a more realistic goal might be to "spend 30 minutes each day practicing mindfulness."

Harness the Power of Technology

In today's digital age, leveraging technology can further enhance the process of setting and tracking your goals. Apps and online platforms provide easy ways to monitor your progress and maintain accountability. Tools like digital calendars, habit trackers, and reminder apps are simple yet effective resources for managing your goals. They allow you to visualize your progress, turning abstract goals into tangible milestones. This visibility enhances motivation and reinforces commitment.

Create a Vision Board or Journal

Visualization techniques also play a crucial role in connecting with your core values. Vision boards, for example, provide a creative outlet to represent your dreams and aspirations visually. By regularly practicing visualization techniques, you reinforce your intentions, internalizing them as part of your daily routine.

Guided visualization exercises and mental imagery are more than just physical boards, and they can be powerful tools for mentally rehearsing your desired outcomes. Just like athletes vividly imagine success to enhance their performance, you can envision achieving your goals to strengthen your resolve and prepare for real-world execution. This bridges the gap between your subconscious desires and conscious actions, ensuring that your intentions translate into meaningful behavior.

If you're juggling a busy professional life, integrating these tools and techniques into your daily routine can turn goal setting from an overwhelming task into a rewarding journey. If you're a parent or going through a significant life change, thoughtfully crafting your goals can provide direction and a sense of renewal. Additionally, modeling positive habits for your children demonstrates resilience and dedication, showing them how to face challenges while staying true to their aspirations.

Creating specific, meaningful goals aligned with your aspirations, and life mission empowers you to rise with intention. Embracing personalized strategies, leveraging modern technology, and using frameworks designed to enhance clarity and focus can help you lay the foundation for sustainable growth and transformation. In a world full of distractions and constant change, grounding yourself in thoughtfully crafted, intentional goals doesn't just lead to success, but also paves the way to a more fulfilling and purposeful life.

Lastly, be open to adjustments. Life is unpredictable, and sometimes, your goals will need to evolve as you grow and learn. If something isn't working, or if new opportunities arise, don't be afraid to adapt to your goals. Remember that progress is more important than perfection. Celebrate every step forward, no matter how small, and appreciate the lessons learned along the way. For example, let's say you're a working parent who values family time and personal growth. You could set a goal to "spend more quality time with my family" by planning one family outing every month for the next year. For health, your goal might be to "work out three times a week for 30 minutes for the next three months, prioritizing activities you enjoy." For financial literacy, you might set the goal to "read one personal finance book every two months for the next year."

Personalized, meaningful goals are those that resonate with your values, passions, and life circumstances. They're specific, achievable, and contribute to your long-term happiness and success. By identifying what matters most to you, breaking your goals into manageable tasks, and staying flexible, you can create a roadmap that leads to fulfillment and growth.

Aligning Intentions With Actions

Aligning your daily actions with clear intentions is key to forming meaningful and lasting habits. This connection bridges the gap between who you aspire to be and how you act every day. It's more than setting lofty goals—it's about turning abstract ideas into practical, everyday practices. But how do you make this a reality? Crafting an action plan gives you direction and sets you on a path to success. Below are a few strategies to align your intentions with your daily actions.

Be Clear About Your Intentions

Clarity is the cornerstone of any effective action plan. Without it, even the most well-intentioned goals can feel overwhelming or out of reach. When you're clear about what you want and how you plan to get there, you create a roadmap that turns abstract ideas into actionable steps. For example, let's say your goal is to become more organized at work. While that's a worthy intention, it's also broad and undefined. The key to progress lies in breaking it down into small, specific, and achievable steps that you can implement consistently.

Start by identifying what "being more organized" looks like in practice. Does it mean clearing the clutter from your desk? Prioritizing tasks more effectively? Reducing time spent searching for important documents? Once you've pinpointed these specifics, you can translate them into daily or weekly actions. For instance, dedicate just ten minutes each morning to declutter your workspace. Whether it's tossing out old notes, filing away documents, or neatly arranging your supplies, this small ritual creates a sense of order that sets a positive tone for the day.

In addition to decluttering, list out your top priorities for the day. Instead of diving into your inbox or tackling tasks at random, spend a few moments creating a simple to-do list or identifying your "big three" tasks—those that are most important to accomplish. This step not only gives you a clear direction but also prevents you from feeling scattered or overwhelmed. Over time, these seemingly small habits build momentum, creating a sense of control and efficiency that directly supports your larger goal.

By breaking a vague desire, like "being more organized," into tangible actions, you can execute each day, and you give your goal structure and purpose. These manageable steps also provide a sense of accomplishment, reinforcing your motivation to keep going. The result of these small actions is increased productivity and efficiency, which supports your success—one small, intentional step at a time.

Practice Self-Assessment

Action plans also encourage accountability. When your intentions translate into clear, concise tasks, tracking progress becomes easier. Regular check-ins—weekly or daily—help you assess whether your actions align with your goals. Ask yourself if your daily activities support your goal of staying organized. If not, what adjustments can you make?

These reflective moments keep you on track and prevent distractions from derailing your progress.

This process of reflection doesn't end with self-assessment. Introducing feedback loops—combining self-reflection and external input—can significantly enhance your growth. Feedback from peers, mentors, or supervisors provides valuable insights you might overlook on your own. For instance, discussing your productivity strategies with a colleague can give you fresh perspectives on improving efficiency. Equally, regularly carrying out a self-assessment helps you recognize your behavior patterns. Are certain habits repeatedly derailing your intentions? Recognizing these patterns is the first step toward making effective changes, propelling you toward your intentional living path.

Employ Habit Staking

One effective way to embed new intentions into your daily routine is habit stacking. This involves linking a new habit to an existing one, ensuring a smoother integration into your daily life. For example, if you intend to practice mindfulness, try pairing it with a habit you've already established, like drinking your morning coffee. Take a few minutes each morning to engage in mindful breathing or reflective thinking. By attaching the new habit to something familiar, the change feels less overwhelming and more sustainable over time.

Additionally, understanding that habits operate within a broader system enhances your flexibility in adapting them. Habit stacking simplifies this process by enhancing existing routines rather than overloading your schedule. It turns daily actions into intentional steps aligned with your long-term goals.

Feedback loops complement this approach by enabling continuous evaluation. After integrating new habits, regular check-ins ensure you stay aligned with your intentions. When misalignments or unexpected challenges arise, these feedback systems help you adapt quickly. For example, if your morning mindfulness practice falters due to a busy schedule, a small adjustment—like setting an earlier alarm—can keep you on track. This adaptability ensures sustained progress, even in the face of obstacles.

Achieving harmony between your intentions and daily actions doesn't happen overnight. It's a gradual process built on consistency and commitment. You may need to tweak your strategies, but every step you take reinforces your identity as someone who actively shapes your destiny.

Ultimately, creating action plans, engaging in regular self-reflection, employing habit stacking, and embracing feedback loops are powerful tools to ensure your daily actions reflect your intentions. Together, they transform aspirations from abstract ideas into achievable realities, fostering a life of purpose and fulfillment.

Embracing Intentional Habits: Your Path to Authentic Growth

Building habits that truly resonate with your core values, rather than chasing fleeting trends, is the key to lasting change. By focusing on intentionality, you create habits that reflect your principles, leading to greater satisfaction and long-term sustainability. When you connect your actions to what genuinely matters to you, every choice you make becomes an expression of your authentic self. This intentional approach not only prevents burnout but also provides a steady anchor, helping you deal with life's challenges while remaining true to who you are.

Remember, habit formation isn't about instant change; it's about steady, thoughtful progress. Each small, deliberate choice adds up, supporting your broader goals and reinforcing your values. Whether you're striving for balance, rebuilding after setbacks, or you're a parent modeling positive behaviors to your kids, intentional habits lead to personal growth and fulfillment. By aligning your actions with your unique values, each step you take becomes part of a lifelong journey toward a more purposeful and rewarding life.

Chapter 3:
Building the Habit Loop

First, forget inspiration. Habit is more dependable. Habit will sustain you whether you're inspired or not. Habit is persistence in practice. –Octavia Butler

Imagine standing at the edge of a pond, holding a small pebble. When you toss it into the water, ripples expand outward, each circle growing larger than the last. Now, think of your habits like that pebble—small actions that send waves through your daily life, impacting everything they touch.

One morning, you choose to start your day with five minutes of gratitude instead of scrolling through your phone. At first, it feels insignificant, but soon, you notice an improvement in your mood. You're more patient with your colleagues, more present with your family, and better equipped to handle challenges. That tiny habit, like the pebble, creates a ripple effect, changing not just your day but your overall outlook.

Building the habit loop is a fascinating process that reveals how you can systematically integrate certain behaviors into your daily life. Think of it as the key to optimizing your routines, where understanding your triggers, routines, and rewards leads to more effective habit formation. If you've ever wondered why some actions stick while others fade away or why you seem to repeat certain patterns effortlessly, this chapter will shed light on these mysteries. By examining the mechanics behind habits, you'll discover how small strategic adjustments can change fleeting intentions into deliberate actions, ensuring they become second nature with minimal conscious effort.

Understanding the key elements of the habit loop—triggers that spark action, routines that provide structure, and rewards that reinforce behavior—can transform the way you build habits. By breaking down the habit loop, you'll gain insight into why certain behaviors repeat and how to harness this cycle to your advantage.

Identifying triggers, whether they're situational cues like a specific time of day or emotional prompts like stress or excitement, is the first step. These triggers signal habits, and recognizing them allows you to consciously shape your actions. For example: pairing a daily task, like brushing your teeth, with a new habit—such as practicing gratitude—can transform simple moments into powerful opportunities for change.

We'll also explore how incorporating time-based triggers, like setting a specific time for exercise, or social triggers, such as partnering with a friend for accountability, can make your new habits more sustainable. These strategies not only make habit-building more effective but also integrate seamlessly into your daily life.

Whether you're managing a busy schedule, striving to set a positive example for your family, or simply looking to create more balance, these insights provide practical tools for lasting change. By leveraging the habit loop and optimizing its components—triggers, routines, and rewards—you'll improve time management, adapt to transitions, and cultivate habits aligned with your long-term goals.

Understanding Triggers in the Habit Loop

Before we get into the details of how to create a habit loop, let's first define what it is. A habit loop is a simple cycle made up of three parts: a trigger, a routine, and a reward. For example, let's say you want to develop a reading habit. The trigger could be setting a specific time each day, like right before bed, to read for 15 minutes. The routine is reading, and the reward could be the sense of relaxation or the feeling of accomplishment you get after finishing a chapter. As you repeat this loop, the habit becomes easier and more automatic.

Understanding triggers is an essential aspect of habit formation. Triggers act as the spark that ignites the habit loop, setting routines in motion and leading to rewards. By learning to identify and optimize these cues, you can cultivate healthier, more effective habits.

Here are a few types of triggers that can motivate you to consistently build a habit.

Contextual Triggers

Contextual triggers play a significant role in habit formation. These are cues embedded in your environment or specific situations that prompt certain actions. Think about walking into a dark room and instinctively turning on the light. This seemingly automatic response is driven by context. Similarly, you can strategically use environmental cues to solidify habits. For instance, placing your gym clothes where you'll see them first thing in the morning can subtly nudge you toward your workout routine without much thought. Recognizing and leveraging the right contextual triggers helps turn intentional actions into effortless routines. Simple adjustments—like placing healthy snacks in plain view instead of hiding them behind **the** bags of chips—can make adopting positive behaviors more natural. By thoughtfully arranging your environment, you create a setting where good habits flourish and integrate seamlessly into your daily life.

Emotional Triggers

Emotional triggers, though often overlooked, have a powerful influence on our actions. These triggers are the feelings or moods that prompt certain behaviors, and they can work in both positive and negative ways. For example, stress eating is a common emotional trigger where the feeling of stress leads to unhealthy eating habits. But by identifying this emotional pattern, you can shift your response to something more constructive. Instead of reaching for comfort food, you might replace that habit with mindfulness practices, like deep breathing or taking a short walk, turning an emotionally charged moment into a chance for positive change.

By recognizing when emotions are steering your habits, you can harness their energy in a way that benefits you. Instead of allowing negative emotions to dictate your actions, you can redirect them toward behaviors that support your goals, turning potential setbacks into opportunities for growth.

Time-Based Triggers

Incorporating time-based triggers into your routine can also be a powerful tool for building lasting habits. These triggers rely on specific times of the day or established routines to prompt actions. Time is perhaps the most common cue for habits. Think about your morning routine: waking up, brushing your teeth, and having breakfast often happen in a sequence driven by time constraints rather than conscious planning. Structuring your daily activities around consistent time-based cues makes it easier to build new habits. For example, setting aside a fixed time each day for a particular task—such as writing, exercising, or meditating—helps anchor that activity in your schedule. This consistency changes it from a deliberate effort into a natural part of your day. Time cues can be invaluable in building routine behaviors, prompting actions even when motivation wavers.

Social Triggers

Social triggers are another compelling force in habit formation; leveraging social dynamics and interactions can reinforce behaviors. As humans, we are inherently social creatures, and our actions are often influenced by the people around us. Having people who share similar goals can strengthen accountability and commitment to habits. For instance, joining a running club or a study group creates a shared experience where mutual encouragement acts as a trigger, motivating you to show up and stay consistent. Social accountability can be a powerful motivator, as knowing someone else is relying on you or expecting your participation encourages follow-through. This reinforces current habits and creates an environment that supports adopting new ones.

While each trigger type—contextual, emotional, time-based, and social—offers its unique benefits, understanding how they work together can significantly enhance the process of forming new habits. Contextual triggers set the stage, emotional triggers provide motivation, time-based triggers create a routine, and social triggers offer accountability. By combining these elements, you can build a robust and effective habit loop. The key is identifying which triggers align best with your lifestyle and goals and then incorporating them into your daily routine.

These insights are especially valuable if you're recovering from setbacks or going through a major life change. Adjusting to new circumstances often requires rebuilding familiar patterns in the face of uncertainty. By focusing on triggers, you can regain control over your behaviors, steering them toward desired outcomes. Whether it's finding comfort in a consistent morning routine during chaotic times or using social interactions to stay connected, triggers provide the structure needed to restore stability.

Understanding and applying triggers can go beyond personal growth and influence family dynamics. If you're a parent, modeling positive behaviors through thoughtfully crafted habit loops sets an example for your kids, teaching them important skills in self-regulation and discipline. Identifying meaningful triggers in a family setting, like shared mealtimes or bedtime routines, creates a harmonious and supportive environment that promotes individual and collective growth.

Structuring Sustainable Routines

The foundation of habit formation lies in the routines—they are the lifeblood of our daily lives, driving the habit loop toward lasting change. Establishing a sustainable routine revolves around one fundamental principle: consistency. But how can we integrate this consistency into our ever-changing lives? It starts with the understanding that repetition breeds familiarity, which eventually leads to automaticity. Consistency doesn't necessarily mean rigidity, but it's about being adaptable in your daily routine. Life is full of surprises that can change your day in an instant. But by learning to adjust your routine when things change, you can maintain your habits without interruption.

Let's look at a few strategies to achieve this.

Set Micro-Habits

Breaking down your routine into smaller, manageable steps is a highly effective approach. Complex habits, such as adopting a healthier lifestyle, can feel overwhelming and difficult to start. By breaking them into micro-habits, the process becomes simpler and more approachable. Each small, consistent action creates momentum, like laying one brick at a time to build a strong structure. For example, instead of attempting to completely overhaul your diet all at once, start with a single micro-habit, such as drinking an extra glass of water each day. This small step establishes a solid foundation, making it easier to gradually introduce larger changes. These incremental improvements are not only more manageable but also trigger frequent dopamine releases, reinforcing the new behavior as positive and rewarding (Strobl, 2023).

Use Habit Stacking

In Chapter 2, we discussed the importance of habit stacking—linking a new habit to an existing one in the process of habit formation. For instance, brushing your teeth is already part of your morning routine. Use that as a cue to add a new habit, such as a two-minute mindfulness practice. The connection between the two activities makes the new habit easier to integrate. Successful individuals often attribute their accomplishments to the practice of habit stacking, steadily enhancing their routines with minimal effort.

Be Flexible in Your Approach

Even the most carefully planned routine requires flexibility. Life is dynamic, and a rigid routine may no longer serve its purpose as circumstances change. Flexibility allows you to adjust your routine to match your circumstances, ensuring it remains effective. For example, if your evening jog becomes inconvenient due to a job change, you might shift to home workouts or another form of exercise. This adaptability helps you maintain the essence of your routine while ensuring it fits your current lifestyle.

Turning negative emotional triggers into positive action cues can significantly enhance the effectiveness of your routine. Often, certain emotions or situations can derail our efforts to maintain consistent habits. For instance, a stressful day at work might tempt you to skip your evening run or indulge in unhealthy snacks. However, by training yourself to recognize these emotional triggers, you can shift them into positive actions. Instead of viewing stress as a barrier, you can treat it as a cue to engage in a calming activity, like deep breathing or journaling. This shift not only strengthens your routine but also turns your emotions into tools for reinforcing desired habits, creating a positive feedback loop that fuels your progress.

Similarly, leveraging positive emotions can solidify your habits. Celebrating your victories, no matter how small they may seem, creates a sense of accomplishment that reinforces the behavior. For example, after completing a week of your new morning yoga routine, reward yourself with something enjoyable and fitting, such as a relaxing bath. Associating achievement with positive feelings amplifies the brain's reward pathways, which strengthens the habit loop and encourages repetition (Strobl, 2023).

Additionally, incorporating time-specific associations into your routine can improve consistency. While not every routine needs to be tied to a specific time of day, creating time-based cues can increase the consistency of the habit loop. A morning routine can prepare you for the tasks ahead, while an evening routine can help you unwind and signal the end of the day. Setting specific times of the day for micro-habits ensures moments of personal growth amid a hectic schedule. Similarly, if you're recovering from a major setback, structuring your days with time-specific habits creates a sense of stability and direction as you move forward.

Reinforcing Habits With Rewards

We often overlook the impact of rewards on building new habits, yet understanding their role can be the key to making positive change last. Immediate rewards are essential for maintaining motivation. Experiencing an instant boost or positive feeling when adopting a new habit can make all the difference. Think about when you go for a run and feel that rush of endorphins right after; it might not shed pounds instantly, but the immediate mood lift can keep you coming back. This highlights the importance of distinguishing between immediate and long-term rewards. While the benefits of most habits, like better health or improved skills, develop over time, the initial moments of joy help bridge the gap.

Let's explore the different types of rewards and their benefits in reinforcing habits.

Personalized Rewards

Not everyone is driven by the same incentives, which is why personalized rewards are so powerful. Each person has unique motivations that fuel their efforts. For some, it might be as simple as enjoying a favorite treat after reaching a milestone. For others, it could mean dedicating time to their favorite hobby. The key lies in experimentation—trying different rewards to discover what genuinely resonates with you. Celebrating small victories isn't just an enjoyable thing to do; it reinforces your progress and keeps the momentum going.

Social Rewards

Imagine working toward building a new habit, but instead of tackling it alone, you have your friends and family to cheer you on. Social rewards add a whole new layer to the process, making everything feel a bit more engaging and a lot less daunting. As humans, we naturally crave connection and belonging, so sharing our wins—big or small—with others can boost our commitment to change. Think about setting a goal with a close friend, like training for a marathon or adopting healthier eating habits. On the days when your motivation is low, their support can pull you through. And when they hit a rough patch, your encouragement could be the push they need. It becomes a team effort, where you celebrate each other's victories and help each other through setbacks. What could have felt like a lonely uphill climb turns into a shared adventure full of camaraderie and connection.

Even little things—like a friend acknowledging your progress or a bit of friendly competition—can add a spark of excitement. Knowing that someone else is invested in your journey makes the whole process more meaningful. Suddenly, your personal milestones aren't just yours; they become shared triumphs. When you have a support system, building new habits feels less like a chore and more like a rewarding, shared experience.

Gamification

Building new habits doesn't have to be a boring process—you can turn it into an engaging adventure! Think of it like setting off on a journey where each step brings something new and exciting. By adding a little creativity and fun, you can turn those everyday routines into something you actually look forward to. For instance, why not gamify your habit-building? Set challenges for yourself, track your progress with fun apps, or reward yourself with small treats when you hit a milestone. It's like turning your goals into a game, where each win gives you that little boost of motivation to keep going.

Aligning Rewards to Personal Values

Now, consider how powerful rewards can be when they align with your values. The right incentive can trigger a rush of dopamine, that feel-good chemical that boosts motivation. It's not just about external prizes; internal drivers like autonomy and skill mastery are equally important. For example, if you're a parent and want to encourage a love of reading in your child. By celebrating each completed book with a special trip to the library or bookstore, you create a rewarding experience that encourages growth and shared joy. Such thoughtful rewards make the habit more meaningful and memorable.

Remember, not every reward will hit the mark, and that's okay—it's all part of the learning process. The real challenge is noticing when an incentive doesn't resonate and being open to making adjustments. Imagine you set a goal to exercise regularly and decide to reward yourself with a weekend hiking trip. But what if you realize that hiking feels more like another chore than a treat? Instead of motivating you, it might leave you feeling drained or unenthusiastic about your progress. In this case, what seemed like a good reward initially could end up backfiring. The key is to stay flexible and choose something that genuinely excites you—maybe a relaxing spa day or a movie night would be a better fit. It's all about finding rewards that feel truly rewarding and keep you energized on your journey.

Creating a balance between immediate and long-term rewards is essential in reinforcing habits. Short-term incentives provide the initial spark, keeping enthusiasm high, while long-term rewards sustain interest and commitment over time. When layered thoughtfully, these rewards turn habits from mundane tasks into dynamic, enriching experiences. They become bridges connecting present actions to future outcomes, ensuring that every step forward feels purposeful and rewarding.

Worksheet: Identifying Personal Triggers and Rewards to Reinforce New Habits

Now that we've explored how to create a habit loop, let's personalize it by identifying what drives and challenges you. Using the example on the worksheet below, reflect on and write down your unique triggers and the rewards that resonate most. By understanding the situations that test your progress and the incentives that keep you motivated, you'll be better equipped to build habits that stick. Tailoring your approach to fit your needs will make the journey more effective—and a lot more enjoyable.

Habit	Trigger	Reward (What reinforces the habit)	How to adjust or use the trigger
Example: Exercise daily	Feeling tired after work	Feeling energized and accomplished	Place workout clothes by the door as a reminder

Applying the Habit Loop

We've uncovered the mechanics of the habit loop, highlighting how triggers, routines, and rewards work together to shape our daily behaviors. Think of the habit loop as the engine driving everything you do. By understanding how each element functions, you can make your habits work for you.

Recognizing which triggers resonate with you—whether contextual, emotional, time-based, or social—can help you create a more personalized and effective approach to building lasting habits.

As we wrap up, take a moment to reflect on how these insights connect with your own. Whether you're balancing work, managing life changes, or a parent striving to lead by example, the habit loop can be life-changing. Creating positive loops with thoughtful rewards will not only reinforce these habits, but also bring joy into the process. It's all about creating a framework that balances consistency with adaptability, ensuring that your habits evolve with you—no matter what life throws at you. This isn't just about changing behaviors; it's about creating an environment where growth feels natural and rewarding.

Remember, having a support system can make all the difference in reinforcing your habits. Involving friends or family can add a social twist to the process. Imagine working toward your goals alongside someone who cheers you on and shares in your victories—it's way more fun than going it alone! The key to developing lasting positive habits is to find what excites you and makes the process feel less like a chore. Whether it's setting up mini-rewards, celebrating small achievements, or turning your progress into a friendly competition, there are endless ways to make habit-building a rewarding adventure. So, why not make the journey as enjoyable as the destination?

Chapter 4:
Start Small, Aim High

The man who moves a mountain begins by carrying away small stones. – Confucius

Big dreams often feel overwhelming at first, but their true power lies in the small, deliberate steps that bring them closer to reality. Every significant achievement starts as an idea, nurtured by simple, manageable actions. These small beginnings build momentum, laying the foundation for progress and cultivating resilience to navigate life's challenges. By starting small, we cultivate sustainable habits, grow intentionally, and turn aspirations into tangible outcomes.

Let's explore how starting small can empower you to stay motivated and focused. We'll explore practical strategies like the "1% Rule" and insights from neuroscience on habit formation, highlighting how these principles promote lasting growth. Setting clear and attainable goals can transform vague aspirations into actionable steps, paving the way for consistent progress. Whether you're working on healthier habits, chasing a personal dream, or embarking on a new career path, this chapter will show you how to harness the power of small steps to achieve remarkable results.

Science of Incremental Progress

When it comes to achieving big goals, starting small isn't just a motivational concept—it's rooted in both psychology and physiology. Breaking down big dreams into small, manageable steps is not only effective but also backed by science. Let's examine how incremental progress transforms even the loftiest aspirations into achievable goals.

Consider the 1% Rule, which emphasizes consistent, incremental improvement. By advancing just one percent daily, exponential growth becomes achievable over time. Imagine you're training for a marathon. Instead of pushing yourself to run 26 miles right from the start, you begin with short jogs, gradually increasing your distance. Each day, you run a little bit more, and by the end of a few weeks, you've significantly improved your stamina. This incremental approach isn't just about building physical endurance—it's also about boosting confidence and cultivating discipline. Each small step reinforces the habit, and over time, these tiny actions snowball into significant progress. The beauty of the 1% Rule is that it shows how real success often comes from making steady, consistent efforts rather than trying to achieve perfection all at once.

This idea of incremental progress is also supported by the concept of neuroplasticity, the brain's ability to reorganize itself and form new neural connections throughout life. Our brains are incredibly adaptable, and small, consistent actions help them adjust, making it easier to form new habits and master new skills. For example, learning a new language can feel daunting at first, but practicing just five minutes a day has a compounding effect. Those daily practices strengthen the neural pathways associated with language learning, and over time, the brain becomes more efficient at processing new words and grammar. Essentially, the brain learns how to learn. Neuroplasticity is a powerful reminder that by consistently making small changes, we can rewire our brains, enabling us to stick to new habits and make progress in seemingly difficult tasks (Kays et al., 2012).

Small, repeated actions are the foundation for building long-lasting habits. Whether you're training for a marathon or learning a new skill, starting small allows your brain to adapt and ensures that the process feels less overwhelming. With each tiny step, you are not just moving toward your goal—you're making the goal itself more achievable, paving the way for sustained success.

The Benefits of Taking Incremental Steps

Starting small supports long-term retention by making changes feel more manageable, which increases your commitment. Large, sudden shifts in your routine can feel overwhelming and discourage you from making progress. However, breaking these changes into smaller, achievable steps keeps you motivated. For example, adopting a healthier diet may feel overwhelming if you attempt to change everything at once. However, starting with one healthy meal or snack a day is more achievable. As these small changes become habits, they build a foundation for broader change. Consistency is key; when you consistently make small adjustments, they become more comfortable, reinforcing new behaviors until they become second nature.

Research demonstrates that specific, small goals are significantly more effective than vague, broad ones for fostering lasting behavioral change (Lee, 2017). Clear, actionable targets provide both focus and measurable outcomes, making it easier to stay motivated. For instance, in a study on exercise routines, participants who set precise, incremental objectives were significantly more likely to stick to their plans than those who simply aimed to get fit (Johnson, 2016). Setting clear goals makes it easier to track progress and allows you to regularly celebrate your milestones, helping you stay motivated.

Studies carried out on the power of specificity further reinforce this idea. In the study, when participants pursued broad, ambitious goals without breaking them down into manageable steps, their commitment and success rates dropped noticeably (Coreen, 2024). In contrast, small, achievable goals acted as guideposts, keeping participants on track toward their larger ambitions. This highlights that smaller steps not only make the journey feel less overwhelming but also ensure steady progress and direction along the way.

If you're juggling a busy schedule, implementing small, manageable changes can be invaluable. Incorporating these simple adjustments into your daily routine can improve your well-being without disrupting your flow. For example, standing during phone calls rather than sitting all day is a quick fix that promotes better health without demanding extra time—an easy yet effective shift. Similarly, if you've faced a major setback, this approach can help you rebuild your life. Starting small can help you regain confidence, proving that steady progress is possible, even when it feels slow.

The same principle holds true in parenting. If you want to model positive habits for your family, simple actions, like reading a chapter of a book each night or going for daily walks, not only enhance personal well-being but also set a powerful example for children. When kids see these small, consistent efforts, they learn valuable lessons about perseverance, patience, and the rewards of gradual progress.

To put these principles into practice, identify an area you wish to improve, then break it down into a small, achievable step that you can address today. Incrementally build upon this foundation, celebrating each step forward. Remember that setbacks are part of the journey—use them as opportunities to learn and adjust your strategies. Even minor progress is still progress; celebrate small wins along the way.

Breaking Down Big Tasks

When starting on the path to an ambitious goal, the idea of taking that first step can feel intimidating. But breaking down big goals into smaller, manageable tasks, also known as goal segmentation, can make the journey much more achievable. It alleviates the overwhelming feeling of tackling a huge task and boosts your motivation by focusing on small, incremental steps. Think of it like climbing a mountain, and it's unlikely you'll reach the top in one giant leap. Instead, climbers plan their route with stops along the way—base camps where they rest, regroup and celebrate small wins. Similarly, when pursuing personal or professional goals, dividing a large task into smaller, more digestible chunks is like setting up those base camps. Each small success not only marks progress but also reignites your energy, pushing you to keep going.

But how exactly do you structure your time around these segmented goals? Effective time allocation techniques are crucial here. Let's look at a few strategies to achieve this.

Time Block Your Day

The beauty of starting small lies in its simplicity. It's not about perfection or overnight success, but it's about building momentum, step by step, until those small efforts transform your life in ways you never imagined. One effective strategy is time blocking—designating specific periods of your day for particular tasks. Think of your day divided into chunks, each dedicated to completing a small task that contributes to a larger goal. This structured approach helps minimize distractions and creates a focused environment, allowing you to tackle each part of the goal efficiently. For example, if you commit to reading one chapter of a book each morning, you'll steadily progress toward finishing it without feeling overwhelmed by the entirety of the text.

Create a Checklist

A checklist is one of the simplest yet most effective tools for improving productivity. Think of it as a roadmap to your goal—a traveler marking off destinations one by one. Each task or action on your list is a destination, and checking them off brings you closer to your ultimate goal. The satisfaction of marking off items provides a small but powerful boost, motivating you to keep moving forward. It helps you stay on track, even when the journey feels long or overwhelming.

Using a checklist not only motivates you through the visual evidence of your progress, but also keeps you organized. It gives clarity about what needs to be done next and ensures you don't lose sight of any critical steps. Rather than keeping everything in your head and risking forgetting important tasks, a checklist lets you focus your energy on what you need to accomplish.

Let's take writing a book as an example. The idea of writing an entire book can be daunting, but breaking it down into manageable steps using a checklist makes it feel much more achievable.

Research and outline:

Research topic thoroughly

Create chapter outline

Brainstorm key points for each chapter

Writing the draft:

Write Chapter 1

Write Chapter 2

Write Chapter 3

Continue through all chapters

Editing and revisions:

Review the first draft for structure and flow

Edit for grammar and clarity

Proofread final draft

Publishing process:

Choose a publishing platform (for example, self-publishing or traditional publishing)

Format the book for print and e-book versions

Design cover art

Submit manuscript

Each of these items is a separate action, and by having them laid out, you know exactly what needs to be done at each step. As you complete each task, you check it off the list, giving you a sense of accomplishment and moving you one step closer to the finish line.

As you progress, you'll feel motivated to keep going because you're visually tracking how far you've come. It reduces the risk of feeling overwhelmed by the enormity of the project because you can clearly see what you've done and what's left. Additionally, checklists provide flexibility. If something unexpected comes up, you can easily adjust the list, making it a dynamic tool for staying on course.

In short, checklists are invaluable for managing tasks, boosting motivation, and providing clarity. They allow you to break down larger goals into actionable steps, keeping your goals organized, manageable, and within reach.

Look at Past Achievements

Another effective step is to reflect on past successes. Reviewing what worked well and identifying which small actions contributed to progress can help chart a course for future efforts. Think of it like using old maps to guide you through new territories—learning from previous experiences provides insight into what will help you move forward. For instance, looking back at a previous project might reveal that regular team check-ins were crucial in meeting deadlines, encouraging you to incorporate those meetings into future projects.

Incorporating these strategies may sound straightforward, but flexibility is key. Goals, much like life itself, aren't static. They evolve, and so should your approach to achieving them. Time blocks might shift, checklists will expand or shrink, and reflections could lead to surprising insights. Adapting quickly to these changes while maintaining a focus on the endgame is vital.

Additionally, keeping things simple is essential. By streamlining your strategies and focusing on the essentials, you create a pathway for consistent advancement. Overcomplicating processes often leads to confusion, hindering progress, and dampening enthusiasm. Clear and manageable steps allow us to move forward steadily, one achievable action at a time.

Starting with small, deliberate actions is not only practical but transformative. These incremental steps offer tangible progress, proving that even the loftiest ambitions are within reach. Each small success—every base camp along the way—builds confidence and brings the ultimate goal into sharper, more attainable focus.

Practical Examples of Scaling Goals

Achieving lofty goals begins with understanding the power of starting small. This approach breaks down overwhelming aspirations into manageable steps, creating a sustainable and achievable path to success. By consistently building on small efforts, you create a solid foundation for long-term growth. Through the following relatable examples in fitness, skill development, and professional growth, you'll see how modest beginnings can lead to significant achievements.

The Fitness Journey

In fitness, the journey often starts with something as simple as a daily walk. Initially, this may seem minimal, but walking regularly improves cardiovascular health, boosts mood, and builds stamina. Over time, you might incorporate jogging or exploring challenging terrains, eventually progressing to activities like marathons or strength training—the secret lies in consistency and setting SMART goals. For example, you could commit to walking 30 minutes daily for the first month and gradually increase duration or intensity.

Learning a New Skill

Similarly, when learning a new skill, starting small ensures sustainable progress. Take learning a new language, for example. Learning a single word or phrase each day might feel insignificant, but over weeks and months, these small steps accumulate into a vast vocabulary. This method not only enhances memory retention but also reduces the strain of learning new material. Tools like apps or flashcards can support daily practice while setting milestones—such as mastering a specific number of words or grasping a key concept—offers motivation and a sense of achievement. Over time, these consistent efforts can lead to conversational fluency or even the ability to write proficiently in a new language. This process highlights the importance of patience and persistence, showing how small, consistent actions can build into substantial expertise.

The Professional Realm

In the professional realm, setting incremental goals is an effective tool for career advancement. One effective example is weekly networking. Building professional relationships takes time, but consistent efforts lay the groundwork for a reliable network. Attending a networking event or arranging a coffee meeting with a new contact weekly may seem small, yet these actions collectively enhance visibility, create opportunities, and provide access to industry insights. Over time, these interactions can lead to meaningful connections, such as mentors, collaborators, or potential employers. Setting measurable goals, like connecting with two new professionals each month or attending one major industry event quarterly, can provide structure and ensure steady growth.

Creative Pursuits

Similarly, creative projects thrive with a step-by-step approach. Tackling a large project, like writing a novel, painting a series, or launching a startup, can feel overwhelming at first. However, focusing on manageable daily tasks—such as dedicating 15 minutes a day to writing or sketching—builds momentum and ensures consistent progress. Over time, these small efforts result in a complete and polished work.

Breaking creative goals into smaller parts and celebrating milestones maintains enthusiasm while preventing burnout. This allows you to be flexible and adaptable, creating space for your creativity to grow without the weight of unrealistic expectations.

Implementing guidelines for each of these areas can further enhance your progress. In fitness, gradual routines reduce the risk of injury while maintaining improvement. For language learning, using techniques like spaced repetition strengthens comprehension and retention. In professional networking, setting clear communication goals and tracking interactions helps optimize effort and build stronger connections. Lastly, for creative projects, creating a structured yet adaptable plan gives you direction and encourages you while cultivating innovation.

Embracing Small Beginnings

Building new habits is a journey and never underestimate the power of small beginnings and their role in achieving significant goals. By embracing the principles of incremental progress and goal segmentation, you pave the way for a more manageable and fulfilling journey toward success. Whether you're balancing the demands of personal and professional life, recovering from a challenging transition, or nurturing positive habits within your family, these small, deliberate steps create a foundation for meaningful change. These small steps make larger goals less intimidating and easier to fit into your daily routine without feeling overwhelming.

Each action, no matter how minor, contributes to a greater whole, turning daunting aspirations into daily practices that align with your values and goals. The momentum you build through consistent effort builds resilience and motivates you to keep going, proving that progress is not about the pace but how persistently you continue working toward your goals. Remember, every small step is a victory in itself, a reminder that the journey toward big dreams begins with the courage to start.

Chapter 5:
Navigating Setbacks and Roadblocks

Success is stumbling from failure to failure with no loss of enthusiasm. –Winston Churchill

Imagine you've been making steady progress toward a new habit, feeling proud of the momentum you've built. Then life throws a curveball—unexpected responsibilities, a rough day, or a lapse in focus—and suddenly, it feels like everything you've worked for is slipping away. These moments can be frustrating but are a natural part of growth. Setbacks are not signs of failure but opportunities in disguise, teaching resilience, adaptability, and perseverance.

Reframing setbacks as valuable lessons can transform your perspective on failure. Examining common roadblocks and the patterns behind them equips you to anticipate and address challenges before they derail your progress.

Adopting a growth mindset means viewing every challenge on your journey to building better habits as more than just a test—it's an opportunity to evaluate your strategies, adjust them, and tailor them to your evolving circumstances. By identifying early signs of fading motivation, addressing self-sabotaging behaviors, and replacing negative self-talk with empowering affirmations, you can stay on track.

Recognizing Patterns in Setbacks

Forming healthier habits is a journey that naturally involves setbacks and obstacles. Successfully navigating these challenges requires understanding and identifying certain patterns and equipping yourself with strategies to address them effectively. This not only helps you manage current difficulties, but also strengthens your ability to maintain long-term personal growth. Let's look at some strategies you use to identify patterns that often lead to setbacks.

Identify Triggers

One key step in this process is identifying triggers that often lead to setbacks. These might include stress at work, lack of sleep, or even specific social situations that reignite old habits. Recognizing these high-risk situations beforehand allows you to counteract them. For instance, if stressful meetings often result in emotional eating, you could prepare healthier snacks in advance or use calming techniques like box breathing to calm your nerves. Anticipating these challenges helps you stay grounded.

Identifying Loss of Motivation

Another key strategy is recognizing when your motivation starts to wane. Motivation naturally fluctuates, but catching its decline early allows you to make adjustments before losing momentum. This might involve reassessing your goals to ensure they align with your values or seeking new sources of inspiration. For instance, if you notice yourself skipping workouts more frequently, joining a class with friends could reintroduce accountability and enjoyment into your routine. By proactively addressing these factors, you can keep moving forward with resilience and purpose.

Notice if You Self-Sabotage

Let's talk about something we all face at some point in our lives: self-sabotage, especially negative self-talk. These critical thoughts can creep in so naturally that we barely notice them, yet they can significantly impact our lives, chipping away at our confidence and distorting our perception of what we can achieve. But here's the good news: with a bit of effort, you can challenge and change those thoughts. Start by identifying moments when you hear that inner critic take over; try replacing negative self-talk with a kind word or positive affirmation. And don't forget to give yourself credit for small wins. Each step forward, no matter how tiny, is proof that you're making progress. By changing your inner dialogue, you cultivate a mindset that supports your goals instead of undermining them.

Practice Self-Reflection

Reflecting on your past experiences can provide valuable insights and help you understand certain patterns and build resilience. Think back to times when you tried to build new habits—what worked and what didn't? Maybe you tend to drop new routines during busy periods or after minor setbacks. Once you see these patterns, you can make changes to avoid them. For example, you could set more realistic goals, learn better time management techniques, or incorporate mindfulness practices to help maintain focus amid chaos. Reflection isn't just about identifying obstacles and challenges; it also helps you recognize the resilience and strength you've built over time.

Practicing reflection regularly can give you even more insight. Journaling is a great tool for identifying triggers, tracking your progress, taking note of setbacks, and creating a personal guide for how to handle challenges in the future. Over time, you can use these reflections as a cheat sheet to remind you of how you've overcome similar obstacles in the past.

The key to dealing with setbacks is preparation and adaptability. By identifying your triggers, recognizing early signs of waning motivation, addressing self-sabotage, and reflecting on your past experiences, you develop a deeper understanding of yourself and your patterns. This awareness empowers you to make informed decisions and adjust your strategies as needed. If you have a busy schedule, this might mean finding ways to integrate strategies that fit seamlessly into your daily routine. If you're a parent or caregiver, these insights will not only help in your personal growth journey, but also in modeling resilience and healthy habits for your children. No matter where you are in life, these strategies can help you approach setbacks as opportunities for growth, and they can strengthen your commitment to achieving your goals.

Embracing Incremental Progress

Creating and sticking to new habits can be challenging, especially when perfectionism gets in the way. It's easy to fall into an all-or-nothing mindset, where you strive for flawless execution and end up feeling defeated when you fall short. The truth is that aiming for perfection often slows down your progress and creates unnecessary stress. Instead, try embracing the idea of progress over perfection, which often leads to real, sustainable growth.

Think of habits as part of a flexible journey rather than a strict set of steps. For example, if you're trying to start a fitness routine, instead of committing to a rigorous daily workout schedule that might feel overwhelming, try starting with just two or three sessions a week. Gradually build from there as you find your rhythm. This adaptable approach allows you to create habits that fit into your life without burning out or giving up.

Embrace Setbacks as a Natural Part of the Process

Setbacks are inevitable, but they're also opportunities to learn and grow. When you encounter challenges, don't view them as failures. Instead, see them as stepping stones that help you identify what's not working and make adjustments. For instance, if you're trying to wake up earlier but keep hitting snooze, look at the root causes. Are you staying up too late? Do you need to prep for your morning the night before? By analyzing what's holding you back, you can refine your strategy and get closer to your goal. Recognizing setbacks as a natural part of the process of developing new habits allows you to give yourself grace and forgive yourself when things don't go as planned. Instead of striving for perfection, celebrate the small wins along the way. Over time, this will boost your motivation and reinforce the importance of flexibility and adaptability in the process of habit formation.

Focus on Consistent Changes

Focusing on small, consistent changes rather than overwhelming shifts can help you build momentum and highlight the power of incremental victories. When you celebrate these small wins, you reinforce your confidence and remind yourself that progress is happening. For example, if you're trying to prioritize self-care, you might set aside just ten minutes each day for relaxation. While it might seem small, this simple act can lead to significant improvements in your overall well-being and productivity over time, proving that steady adjustments add up to meaningful results.

Practice Self-Compassion

To overcome perfectionistic tendencies, try incorporating self-compassion as a daily habit. Often, setbacks trigger negative self-talk, which can derail progress. Cultivating a kinder, more forgiving internal dialogue helps counteract self-criticism and builds resilience. Self-compassion involves recognizing shared human imperfections and treating yourself with empathy. To practice self-compassion, try writing positive affirming letters to yourself or practicing mindfulness meditations to establish a supportive mindset, making it easier to sustain momentum. For example, if you're struggling with work-life balance and feel defeated by setbacks, instead of succumbing to self-blame, reframe the narrative to acknowledge your efforts. Adapting your strategies can turn the situation into a learning experience. This compassionate approach encourages persistence, transforming obstacles into opportunities for growth.

The importance of self-compassion becomes especially clear when you consider how negative self-perceptions can hold you back. Imagine you've just started working on a new work-life balance strategy, but you struggle to stick to it. Instead of showing yourself grace, you might find yourself thinking, "I'm so undisciplined," which only adds to your stress and drains your motivation. Now, imagine changing that narrative. What if you acknowledged your efforts, reminded yourself that setbacks are normal, and encouraged yourself to try again? By approaching challenges with kindness and understanding, you turn obstacles into opportunities for growth, making it much easier to stay on track and build lasting habits.

Set SMART Goals

Avoiding the all-or-nothing mentality starts with setting realistic and achievable goals, which is key to overcoming perfectionism. You can use the SMART framework—specific, measurable, achievable, realistic, and timely—to guide you in this process. By creating specific and attainable objectives, you take the pressure off yourself to meet impossible standards and instead focus on making progress through manageable steps. For example, if you're aiming to improve your family's nutrition, you might start by introducing one healthy meal per week rather than trying to overhaul everyone's diet overnight. This approach keeps your efforts aligned with what's realistic, helping you build momentum and celebrate your progress along the way.

Breaking down larger goals into smaller, actionable steps is a powerful way to overcome perfectionist tendencies that stem from an overwhelming fear of making mistakes. By focusing on one manageable piece at a time, you reduce overthinking and create opportunities for immediate progress. This not only minimizes stress but also keeps momentum going. Additionally, setting reasonable time limits for tasks can help curb procrastination, which is often rooted in perfectionism. With clear deadlines in place, you'll find it easier to complete tasks without getting caught in the trap of endless revisions.

Lastly, acknowledging and celebrating every achievement, no matter the size sustains motivation and reinforces commitment. Simple practices like journaling your achievements or rewarding oneself for reaching milestones nurture self-esteem and link effort to meaningful outcomes, fueling the drive for continued growth.

Bouncing Back From Setbacks

Setbacks are an inevitable part of building lasting habits, but they don't have to be the end of the road. In fact, setbacks can be some of your greatest teachers. When you take a step back to reflect on what went wrong, you're not just analyzing a failure—you're creating a blueprint for future success.

Think about Steve Jobs. His Apple Lisa computer flopped, but instead of letting that define him, he studied the failure, learned from it, and used those lessons to create game-changing innovations like the iPhone (Poor, 2023). Or consider Malala Yousafzai, who turned her near-death experience into a global movement for education and human rights (Blumberg, 2024). These stories remind us that setbacks don't have to be endings—they can be the spark for something even greater if you approach them with curiosity and courage.

On a personal level, reflecting on your own setbacks can be quite insightful. Honest introspection helps you identify patterns, pinpoint areas for improvement, and understand what might be holding you back. One helpful tool is having an adversity journal. Write down each setback, along with how it made you feel and what thoughts ran through your mind at the time. Over time, you'll start to notice recurring themes or triggers. This not only helps you grow but also builds resilience, giving you the clarity to tackle future challenges with confidence.

Reflection shouldn't end with identifying what went wrong—it's about digging deeper to uncover actionable insights that can shape your next steps. When you take the time to review and analyze your setbacks, you arm yourself with the tools to approach future challenges with confidence and strategy. For instance, businesses often use SWOT analysis (strengths, weaknesses, opportunities, and threats) to evaluate challenges and plan their next move. You can apply a similar framework in your personal life to systematically break down setbacks and create solutions that build resilience and adaptability instead of fear.

Turning Setbacks Into Learning Opportunities

Sharing stories of resilience is equally powerful. These aren't just tales of triumph; they're lifelines connecting people through shared experiences. When you open up about your struggles and how you overcame them, you foster a sense of community and mutual support. Hearing others' stories of persistence reminds you that you're not alone—setbacks are universal. By creating a space where collective wisdom flows, you encourage others to share their journeys, building a cycle of empathy, motivation, and growth.

The role of community support in overcoming setbacks can't be overstated. Talking about challenges with others brings fresh perspectives and solutions you might never have considered. More importantly, it nurtures a culture of empathy and understanding, helping you face difficulties with renewed strength. Knowing that others have been where you are—and made it through—offers reassurance and inspires you to keep moving forward, even when the road feels uncertain.

The Role of Self-Compassion

Developing self-compassion is another key element of building resilience. Treat yourself as you would a close friend facing tough times—with kindness, patience, and understanding. This shift in mindset softens the blow of setbacks and reframes them as opportunities for growth, rather than insurmountable failures. With self-compassion, you're better equipped to bounce back stronger, both mentally and emotionally.

Finally, learning from real-world examples of resilience can deepen your understanding of how to deal with setbacks. Consider Netflix: when faced with declining DVD rentals, the company pivoted to online streaming—a bold move that faced criticism but ultimately revolutionized the industry (Westberg, 2024). Their story shows how setbacks can lead to innovation and unforeseen success when met with adaptability and perseverance. Whether in your personal life or on a broader scale, setbacks are often just the starting point for something greater.

Embracing Growth and Progress

Setbacks when trying to adopt new habits are an inevitable part of the journey, but they are also powerful opportunities for growth and resilience. By identifying triggers and patterns—whether they are stress, social pressures, or waning motivation—you can better prepare for these challenges. Reflecting on past experiences allows you to learn valuable lessons and design strategies to avoid repeating similar pitfalls. Developing self-awareness empowers you to approach setbacks with a proactive mindset, reducing their impact and building adaptability. Whether you're managing a demanding schedule, recovering from life changes, or a parent modeling resilience for your family, these insights are invaluable in creating a sustainable path forward.

Embracing setbacks as learning opportunities helps shift your focus from striving for perfection to making progress. Celebrating small victories along the way strengthens positive habits and encourages continuous growth. It's easy for the inner critic to take over when we face setbacks, but incorporating self-compassion can quiet that negative voice, cultivating a healthier and more supportive mindset. Building a support network is also key; being part of a community reminds you that you're not alone in your struggles, offering fresh perspectives and motivation to keep going. When you focus on progress instead of perfection, you create an environment where meaningful, lasting change becomes not just possible but truly rewarding.

Chapter 6:
Creating a Support System

You have to rely on your support system. Growing up, I always thought it was a sign of weakness to ask for help, but now I realize it's really a sign of strength to say, 'I need help, I can't do it all. –Kerri Walsch

Imagine standing at the base of a mountain, ready to climb. You have your gear, your map, and your determination—but you're missing one crucial thing: a guide. This guide isn't just someone who knows the path; they help you when the trail gets rough, point out hidden dangers, and encourage you when the summit feels far away. That's exactly what a support system does when you're building new habits. It offers you accountability, motivation, and the wisdom of shared experiences. Whether it's friends cheering you on, family members offering a listening ear, or a mentor sharing valuable insights, your network can be the difference between stumbling and soaring.

Building a support system is essential for developing new habits, offering the structure you need to stay on track. Your support network acts as an anchor when life gets busy, offering accountability, guidance, and feedback to help you stay consistent and motivated. Whether it's close friendships, family members, professional mentors, or a community group, each relationship adds a valuable layer of support to help you stick to your new routine and achieve your goals. To make the most of your support system, focus on building relationships that balance positivity with constructive feedback. Surround yourself with people who inspire you, celebrate your progress, and help you refocus when things get tough. By actively leaning on these connections, you'll find it easier to stick to your new routines and grow into the person you're striving to become.

The Power of Accountability Partners

An accountability partner can be a game-changer when working to build new habits. This person helps you stay focused and motivated, acting as a support system to keep you aligned with your goals, especially when challenges arise. By sharing your progress with them, you create a sense of responsibility—not just to yourself but to someone else—which can strengthen your commitment.

When you choose to share your goals with an accountability partner, those personal aspirations turn into shared experiences. You're no longer tackling them alone. Instead, it becomes a journey you take together, with mutual encouragement and support helping you stay on track. This collaborative dynamic makes sticking to new habits feel less overwhelming and more rewarding. But here's the key: it's crucial to pick the right accountability partner. Look for someone whose values align with yours and who understands your "why." A great partner doesn't just remind you to follow through—they genuinely get your goals and can provide advice and encouragement tailored to your needs. Without this alignment, the partnership might feel forced or even unhelpful. The right partner helps you grow, bringing synergy to your habit-building process.

To get the most out of having an accountability partner, it's important to set clear agreements right from the start. Decide how often you'll check in, how you'll communicate, and any shared goals or commitments that will strengthen the partnership. Regular check-ins help you track progress, discuss challenges, and adjust your approach as needed.

For those juggling busy schedules—balancing work, school, or personal responsibilities—an accountability partner offers stability and flexibility. For example, you might schedule bi-weekly coffee meetups or quick video calls to stay on track. These regular interactions aren't just about accountability; they can also be a refreshing pause in your routine to refocus and recharge. Imagine you and a friend committing to building healthier habits, like exercising regularly. You could agree to text each other after every workout for encouragement. Over time, this could turn into attending a fitness class together or going for a hike on weekends. Not only does this help you stay consistent with your goals, but it also strengthens your connection and makes the process more enjoyable. If you're going through a big life change or recovering from a setback, an accountability partner can provide much-needed direction and encouragement. Set realistic goals together, celebrate small wins, and establish weekly check-ins to review progress and refine your approach. Having a support system ensures that your efforts remain relevant and effective, no matter how life shifts around you.

However, keep in mind that there's a fine line between helpful accountability and relying too much on external motivation. While having an accountability partner can boost your efforts, it's essential to ensure the partnership fuels your intrinsic motivation rather than replacing it. External motivators, like check-ins or shared goals, can be great for starting a habit, but long-term success relies on your inner drive and self-discipline. When choosing an accountability partner, look for someone who encourages and strengthens your internal motivation without overshadowing it.

A smart approach combines different types of accountabilities, such as personal reflection, community engagement, and technology. While your accountability partner provides encouragement and real-time feedback, apps or digital tools can help you track your progress consistently. Additionally, participating in group activities or community challenges can create a sense of shared responsibility and increase your determination to stick with your goals. Balancing these methods allows you to build habits that are supported by others but ultimately driven by your commitment.

Finding the Right Mentors and Community Guidance

Finding the right mentor or community is essential for personal growth. A mentor offers personalized guidance rooted in real-world experience, often surpassing what you can learn from books or online resources.

Here are a few strategies to help you find a mentor or community support group that will help you achieve your goals.

Find Someone Who Aligns With Your Goals

To find the right mentor, focus on someone whose achievements align with your goals and values. Don't hesitate to reach out—they've likely faced similar challenges and can help you navigate obstacles, avoid common mistakes, and seize growth opportunities. For instance, if you're a young professional struggling to balance work and personal life, connecting with someone who's already mastered that balance can provide you with proven strategies and motivation to stay on track.

Set Clear Expectations

It's also important to set clear expectations and communication methods with your mentor to keep the relationship productive. Their insights can inspire new ideas, help you push past setbacks, and keep you focused on your goals. By leveraging their wisdom, you can accelerate your progress and gain a deeper understanding of what it takes to succeed.

Join a Support Group

In addition to mentorship, tapping into the power of a community can supercharge your efforts. Communities offer shared experiences, diverse perspectives, and a sense of belonging that helps reinforce your commitment to new habits. Whether you join a local running club or participate in online forums for self-improvement, seeing others' successes can fuel your determination. The collective energy of a group working toward similar goals is a powerful motivator that fosters consistency and resilience.

Participating in shared initiatives—such as fitness challenges, neighborhood clean-ups, or book clubs—helps you build new habits while benefiting from the encouragement and accountability of others. Watching how others approach similar goals can provide fresh insights and innovative strategies, making your habit-building journey more engaging and sustainable.

To build lasting habits, creating a well-rounded support system with mentors, peers, and role models is key. This network surrounds you with people who inspire, challenge, and motivate you. Your mentors offer guidance and direction based on their experience, peers provide camaraderie and mutual encouragement, and role models give you a clear vision of the success you're working toward. Together, these layers of support keep you grounded and focused throughout your growth journey.

Maintaining accountability over time within your support system is another vital aspect. Regular check-ins—whether with your mentor or peer group help you track your progress and prevent lapses as you work toward developing new habits. Setting aside time to meet and discuss your achievements, setbacks, and strategies creates accountability, helps you stay motivated, and provides a platform for problem-solving. You can even create formal accountability agreements to strengthen your commitment to your goals.

Don't forget to tap into community resources as well. Many local and online communities offer free workshops, webinars, and networking events that can boost your progress. These resources provide valuable strategies and tools you might not have considered while also expanding your support network. Staying engaged in these opportunities keeps you connected to like-minded individuals and exposes you to fresh ideas, amplifying your ability to stick to and build lasting habits.

Mapping Personalized Support Systems

When you're working on building new habits, creating a support system tailored to your needs is essential. Start by reflecting on your challenges and identifying what type of support you need to overcome them. Think about your past experiences: When have you felt encouraged or stuck? What kinds of support helped you move forward, and what might have been missing? For example, if you struggle to stay motivated to exercise regularly, you might need someone who can offer emotional encouragement or practical advice. Take a close look at your existing relationships and analyze who in your network could be a motivator, advisor, or accountability partner. To help you in this process, I've created the following workbook to help you map out your personalized support system.

Worksheet: Mapping Out Your Personal Support System

Step 1: Identify Your Goal(s)

Write down the habit(s) you want to develop. Be specific. For example: "Exercise for 30 minutes, five days a week" or "Meditate for 10 minutes every morning."

What is your main habit-building goal?

_____
_____

Why is this goal important to you? (Your "why")

_____
_____

Step 2: Reflect on Your Needs

Think about the type of support you need to succeed. Check all that apply and add notes:

Type of support	Do you need this?	Notes: What does this look like for you?
Emotional encouragement	Yes/No	Example: A cheerleader who motivates me when I'm down.
Practical advice	Yes/No	Example: Someone with experience who can guide me.
Accountability	Yes/No	Example: A friend to check in on my progress.
Shared goals/partnership	Yes/No	Example: Someone who's working on the same habit.

| Inspiration (role models) | Yes/No | Example: People who've succeeded in similar goals. |

Step 3: Analyze Your Current Support System

Think about your existing relationships—friends, family, coworkers, or mentors. List people who can play a role in supporting your new habit.

Name	Potential role	Strengths they bring
Example: Sarah	Accountability partner	Reliable, positive, works on fitness, too.

Step 4: Fill the Gaps

If you identified missing roles or areas where you need more support, list ideas to fill those gaps:

Can you ask someone from your network for help? Who?

_____

_____

Can you join a community group, class, or online forum? Where?

_____

_____

Are there digital tools or apps that could provide support? List any here

_____

_____

Step 5: Visualize Your Support System

Draw your support map below. Place yourself in the center and add the names or resources you've identified, along with their roles. Use lines or arrows to show connections.

Example: Draw circles with "Me" in the center, adding Sarah (accountability partner), an app (digital support), or a mentor nearby.

Step 6: Set Clear Expectations

To ensure your support system is effective, establish clear expectations with your accountability partners or mentors:

What will check-ins look like? (Frequency, method)

_____
_____

What type of feedback or encouragement do you need?

_____
_____

What goals or progress will you report?

_____
_____

Step 7: Track Your Progress and Celebrate Wins!

As you move forward, reflect weekly:

Who supported you this week? How?

What small wins did you achieve?

Are there gaps you still need to address?

As you nurture your support ecosystem, remember that it's a dynamic structure, not a fixed one. Regularly evaluating and fine-tuning your network ensures that it remains relevant and effective as your needs and life circumstances evolve. Schedule evaluations based on your milestones—whether monthly, quarterly, or as goals are achieved—to reflect on what's working and what isn't.

Pay close attention to feedback from your support group; their insights can reveal gaps or issues you might overlook. For instance, if an accountability partner seems overwhelmed or disengaged, it may signal the need to redistribute responsibilities or recruit additional support. Equally important is self-reflection—consider whether your needs have shifted. Perhaps you initially needed encouragement, but now benefit more from practical advice or mentorship. Leveraging feedback loops from trusted mentors can further enrich this process. By viewing change as a strength, not a setback, you create a support system that thrives on adaptability. This flexible approach helps you remain steady in the face of life's challenges while staying committed to personal growth.

Finally, remember that strong support systems are built on reciprocity. Encouraging or offering advice to others in your network fosters mutual trust and resilience. This creates a positive cycle in which everyone benefits, ensuring your support system remains a source of strength, even during setbacks.

Building a Support System That Lasts

Building a support network can make a huge difference when it comes to building new habits. Sharing your goals with people who understand where you are in your growth journey and who align with your values and challenges turns what can feel like a solo effort into a shared journey. It could be coworkers motivating each other to hit fitness milestones, friends swapping tips for sticking to a meditation routine, or parents trading hacks for smoother family schedules. These partnerships add a layer of commitment, encouragement, and personalized advice that speaks to where you are.

But it doesn't stop there—getting involved in community groups or using tech tools like habit-tracking apps can level up your support network. The combination of human connection and smart tools gives you a well-rounded, flexible approach to staying on track. With that said, it's all about balance. External motivators—like partners or feedback from a group—are fantastic for getting you started, but the real magic happens when you tap into your own internal drive. By blending different forms of accountability, you create a support system that can adapt when life inevitably shifts. And remember, this isn't just about checking goals off a list; it's about building a resilient, sustainable system where teamwork, self-discipline, and growth go hand in hand. Ultimately, these changes become part of your daily life—effortlessly integrated into the way you live and thrive.

Chapter 7:
Sustainable Momentum

The rhythm of daily action aligned with your goals creates the momentum that separates dreamers from super-achievers. –Darren Hardy

We've all been there. It's January, and you're buzzing with excitement over a fresh goal—hitting the gym three times a week, committing to a healthier diet, or reading daily to expand your knowledge. The first few weeks, you're unstoppable. You can practically feel your future self cheering you on as your routines feel invigorating, your energy is at its peak, and success seems inevitable. Each morning, you spring out of bed, ready to tackle the day and stick to your plan.

But then February rolls around, and reality starts to set in. That initial spark of motivation dims. The gym feels like a chore instead of a challenge, that healthy meal prep starts to feel repetitive, and the book on your nightstand gathers more dust than progress. Suddenly, you're skipping sessions, making excuses, and telling yourself, "I'll get back on track tomorrow." Before you know it, your shiny new goal feels out of reach, leaving you frustrated and stuck.

Why does this happen? Building lasting habits isn't about starting strong—it's about keeping them alive and meaningful over time. Motivation may kickstart your journey, but it's consistency and adaptability that will carry you to the finish line. Habits that feel exciting at first can become stale or even burdensome if you don't take the time to adjust and stay engaged. The good news is it doesn't have to be this way.

What if your routines could evolve with you, growing stronger instead of fading away? Striking a balance between consistency and adaptability is the secret to making your goals not just survive but thrive. When you learn how to inject variety into your routines, tweak your approach as needed, and embrace flexibility without losing focus, you unlock the ability to stay engaged for the long haul.

How can you maintain momentum after the honeymoon phase of your goals fades? How can you keep showing up, even when life throws curveballs? And most importantly, how can you ensure that the habits you build don't just serve you for a season but for a lifetime? Let's explore the tools, strategies, and mindset shifts that can help you maintain momentum, adapt when needed, and turn your short-term efforts into long-term success. It's time to ensure your goals don't just survive—they thrive.

Keeping Habits Fresh and Engaging

To keep your habits engaging over time, adding variety to your routine is essential. Shaking things up helps prevent boredom and the feeling of going through the motions that often lead to abandoning habits altogether. For example, if fitness is your focus, alternate between activities—swap a gym session for a hike, try out a dance class, or explore yoga. If you want to learn a new skill, switch between reading, listening to podcasts, or watching educational videos. This not only keeps your motivation high but also sparks creativity as you explore different facets of the same habit.

Let's explore other strategies you can use to maintain momentum.

Evaluate Your Routine

Every couple of weeks, or maybe once a month, take a step back to evaluate what's working and what needs to be adjusted. Then, add a new twist. Maybe you swap your usual morning jog for a bike ride or change the podcast lineup in your learning routine. Mixing things up not only keeps it fun but also challenges your brain in new ways, which helps you stay interested and engaged with your goals.

Set Mini Goals

Breaking big goals into smaller, bite-sized steps can make a world of difference. Mini goals focus your attention on achievable, short-term objectives, making long-term goals feel more manageable. For instance, if you aim to read more, set a mini goal like finishing one chapter daily or one book monthly. These smaller, bite-sized goals make it easier to take action and maintain momentum without getting bogged down by the enormity of your original goal. They also create opportunities for quick wins, which are incredibly motivating. Each mini goal you accomplish reinforces the belief that you're making progress, and these small victories help keep your confidence high. Instead of thinking of your goal as one massive hurdle, you'll see it as a series of smaller challenges that are more attainable, making the whole process feel much more rewarding.

Celebrate Your Achievements

Every time you accomplish a mini goal, no matter how small it may seem, it's important to acknowledge your success. Celebrating these small wins can significantly boost your motivation and create a positive feedback loop that propels you forward. For instance, after you finish that chapter or hit a milestone in your goal, take a moment to celebrate. You could treat yourself to a favorite snack, enjoy a quick break, or mark the accomplishment visibly, like checking it off a list or updating a progress tracker. These small celebrations aren't just about indulging; they also reinforce the idea that progress, no matter how incremental, is valuable and worthy of recognition. When you celebrate, you build positive associations with the process of working toward your goal, making it more enjoyable and less like a chore. These rewards keep the process satisfying and help maintain a sense of accomplishment as you work your way toward the larger goal.

Use Visual Reminders

Visual reminders are an often-overlooked tool that can make a big difference in keeping you focused on your goals. By having constant visual cues around your home or workspace, you reinforce your intentions and keep your goal at the forefront of your mind. This could be as simple as writing motivational quotes or reminders of your goals on sticky notes and placing them where you'll see them regularly, such as on your desk, mirror, or refrigerator. Alternatively, you could use phone apps, like a habit tracker or a calendar alert, to send reminders throughout the day. The key is consistency—seeing these reminders regularly helps to keep your goal fresh in your mind and encourages you to take action. Although they might seem small or insignificant, these visual prompts can have a powerful effect on your mindset, subtly reinforcing your commitment and nudging you in the right direction. The visual aspect of a goal serves as a constant reminder of your intentions, which can help make the process of habit-building or goal-achieving a more automatic part of your day-to-day life.

Share Your Journey

One of the best ways to keep up your momentum is by getting others involved. Think about it—when you share your goals with a group, there's an extra layer of accountability that's hard to ignore. Whether you join a club, hop onto an online forum, or just share your journey with your friends and family, engaging with a community adds support, encouragement, and even some great ideas you might not have thought of. Imagine you're trying to stick to a running routine. Running alone might work for a while, but joining a local running group can make the entire experience more fun. You'll get the friendly push to show up and the inspiration to keep going when you feel less motivated. Surrounding yourself with people on a similar journey keeps you connected to your "why" and gives you a built-in team of cheerleaders.

To make the most of it, try setting up regular check-ins—weekly, biweekly, or whatever works for your group. It could be virtual or in person, but the idea is to share your progress, talk through challenges, and celebrate wins together. These check-ins turn your goals into a shared experience, and the support you give and receive will make your long-term habits feel less isolating. Before you know it, you'll be trading tips, swapping stories, and finding fresh motivation in the energy of your community.

Strategies to Prevent Burnout

Burnout creeps in gradually, often disguised as everyday stress. At first, you might feel constantly tired, no matter how much rest you get. Tasks you once enjoyed start to feel like chores, and motivation slips away. You might even notice an empty feeling or a sense of detachment from your goals. These are all subtle warning signs of burnout. The good news is if you know what to look for, you can catch it early and take action before things spiral.

Here are some strategies to help prevent burnout and keep you motivated to achieve your goals.

Incorporate Downtimes

Sticking to new habits is great, but you can't go full speed forever. Just as a car needs fuel stops on a long road trip, your mind and body need regular moments of downtime to recharge. These pauses are essential for ensuring that you don't burn out. Breaks don't just mean stopping and resting—they're an opportunity to reset and refresh. Whether it's taking a short breather during the day to stretch or walk, enjoying a weekend activity you love, or taking a longer vacation to fully disconnect, these moments of rest give you the energy needed to continue moving forward. When planned intentionally, they act as a reset button for your mental and physical well-being, allowing you to return to your tasks with renewed focus and vigor. Downtime, when used properly, helps you avoid burnout and maintain the stamina to pursue your goals for the long haul.

Set Realistic Goals

Ambition can be a powerful motivator, but setting goals that are too lofty or too fast can quickly lead to burnout. It's easy to get excited about big goals, but when they feel unattainable, they can quickly overwhelm you. Instead of aiming for perfection, try breaking your goals down into smaller, realistic milestones that feel achievable and rewarding. Think of it like hiking toward a mountain peak—you wouldn't try to scale the entire mountain in one go. You'd take it one step at a time, pausing when necessary, adjusting your route when the terrain gets tough, and celebrating the smaller victories along the way. This approach helps you stay motivated, prevents burnout, and keeps you grounded in the progress you're making, even if it feels slow at times. Progress, no matter how small, is still progress. By setting smaller, attainable goals and giving yourself the flexibility to adjust, you're more likely to stay on course without feeling discouraged.

Cultivate a Positive Mindset

Your mindset is one of your greatest assets when it comes to avoiding burnout. The key is not to ignore challenges, but to approach them with a constructive attitude. Focusing on progress instead of perfection helps you view each step as a win. Simple affirmations like, "I'm making progress, no matter how small," or "Every effort counts" can be incredibly powerful in shifting your perspective. These reminders help you keep negativity in check and prevent you from getting stuck in a cycle of self-doubt. Instead of viewing setbacks as failures, you'll begin to see them as opportunities to learn and grow. Your mindset becomes your shield, allowing you to stay focused on your long-term goals while handling the inevitable ups and downs of the journey. By training your mind to focus on growth, not perfection, you'll maintain the resilience needed to keep going.

Lean on Others For Support

Building resilience and avoiding burnout isn't something you have to do alone. Surrounding yourself with a supportive network of people can make a significant difference in your journey. Whether it's friends, family, or colleagues who understand your goals and challenges, having someone to lean on during tough times can help lighten the emotional burden. Regularly sharing your progress, struggles, and victories with people you trust not only reinforces accountability, but also provides fresh perspectives and encouragement. Having a strong support system helps keep you motivated, especially during moments of doubt or frustration. You're less likely to succumb to burnout when you know that others are there to cheer you on, offer advice, or simply listen. A supportive network can keep you grounded, remind you of your strengths, and help you keep moving forward when the path feels hard to walk alone.

Let Go of Perfectionism

Perfectionism is one of burnout's sneakiest accomplices. The desire for flawless results can create unnecessary pressure and exhaustion, leaving you feeling stuck and overwhelmed. Instead of striving for perfection, focus on progress. Celebrate the small victories and recognize that mistakes and imperfections are a natural part of the process. The journey isn't always smooth, and that's okay. When you embrace the bumps and detours, you'll be able to enjoy the process more and find satisfaction in the effort itself, not just the end result. Perfectionism often leads to frustration and burnout, while focusing on progress allows you to appreciate each step along the way. By accepting that imperfections are part of growth, you'll find it easier to stay motivated and maintain momentum without feeling like you're constantly falling short.

Re-Evaluating Your Habits

Keeping your habits on track takes more than just discipline; it requires regular check-ins and thoughtful adjustments. To maintain sustainable momentum, you need to make sure your habits are still aligned with your personal goals and serving their purpose. One of the best ways to do this is by building in time for reflection. Set aside regular moments—weekly, monthly, or whatever works for you—to pause and evaluate your progress. Use this time to ask yourself: Are my habits helping me move toward my goals? What's working well, and what's not? These self-assessment sessions give you the chance to spot patterns and make tweaks where needed. Whether it's changing the timing of a habit, adjusting your strategy, or identifying obstacles, this intentional reflection ensures your habits stay relevant and effective.

During your reflective sessions, it's helpful to ask yourself key questions: Are my habits effectively driving me toward my goals? What emotions have surfaced during this process? How do I respond to obstacles or challenges? Reflective questions encourage deeper understanding and can help you identify where you need to make changes. To take this process further, consider keeping a journal to record thoughts and insights from these reflections. Writing down your thoughts and insights can be a powerful tool—it gives you a clear record of your progress, provides motivation when you feel stuck, and acts as a guide for future changes. Journaling isn't just about venting frustrations; it's a way to track patterns and refine your approach over time.

Seek Feedback

Another great way to enrich this process is by getting feedback from people you trust—friends, mentors, or colleagues. Sometimes, an outside perspective can help you see blind spots or offer ideas you hadn't considered. Trusted individuals can challenge assumptions, cheer you on, and suggest new strategies. You might schedule regular check-ins, like a bi-weekly coffee with a mentor or a monthly brainstorming session with a group of peers. These conversations can keep you accountable while offering fresh insight, which makes your reflection process even more well-rounded. Remember, the goal here isn't to overhaul everything at once. Small, consistent changes are usually more effective—and sustainable—than big, drastic shifts. Even slight tweaks can help fine-tune your habits and keep you on track.

Be Adaptable

As you work toward your goals, remember to stay flexible. Life is unpredictable, and it's okay for goals to evolve over time. Flexibility doesn't mean giving up or lowering your standards—it's about adapting to your circumstances while keeping your ambitions realistic and achievable. Break big goals into smaller milestones along the way. Not only do these mini-wins give you a reason to celebrate, but they also build momentum, making long-term progress feel less overwhelming.

Celebrate Your Wins

Taking time to celebrate your successes can fuel your momentum and strengthen your commitment. It's about reinforcing the positive habits you're building and creating a cycle of motivation. For example, if your goal is to write a book, celebrate after completing each chapter. The reward doesn't have to be extravagant; it could be something simple like treating yourself to your favorite meal, taking a day off, or enjoying a relaxing activity. At the same time, setbacks are part of the journey. Instead of viewing them as failures, see them as learning opportunities. Take a step back and reflect with compassion—ask yourself what didn't work and why. Maybe a habit fell through because of poor time management, lack of motivation, or unrealistic expectations. Use this information to adjust your approach rather than beating yourself up. For instance, if you struggle to exercise three times a week, you might try shorter workouts or invite a friend to keep you accountable. Learning from what doesn't work helps you adapt and grow.

Embrace Failure as Part of the Process

Failure isn't the opposite of success—it's part of the process. When you embrace failure as a tool for growth, it builds resilience and helps you adapt to challenges. Through self-reflection, identify what you can improve, shift, or let go. This mindset allows you to draw lessons and valuable insights from setbacks. For example, if a particular habit didn't stick, take a closer look at the root cause. Maybe you need a more manageable routine or a better strategy that fits your lifestyle. When you approach failure with curiosity instead of self-criticism, it becomes easier to tweak your methods and keep moving forward.

Set Milestones

Breaking down big goals into smaller, measurable milestones can make even the most overwhelming tasks feel doable. Milestones act like checkpoints, giving you clear targets to hit and helping you monitor your progress along the way. For instance, if you're working on a large project, set specific mini-goals—like completing one section or finishing a draft—and celebrate those achievements as you go. Visual tools, such as progress charts or tracking apps, help you track progress and identify areas for adjustment. These constant reminders of progress keep you focused and motivated.

Building Momentum: Turning Small Wins Into Lasting Progress

Keeping your habits fresh and engaging is the secret of turning routines into lifelong commitments. Variety and adaptability are your best allies—whether that's changing up your workouts, trying new learning methods, or approaching tasks with a fresh perspective. This not only wards off boredom, but also reignites creativity and motivation.

Celebrate every milestone, no matter how small, and lean on your community for support. Surrounding yourself with positive reinforcement, using visual progress trackers, and sharing your wins with others can turn even the most mundane habits into meaningful achievements.

Remember, challenges are part of the journey. Embrace flexibility and see setbacks as opportunities to learn and grow. Regularly reflect on your habits, make timely adjustments, and ensure they align with your bigger goals. Above all, strike a balance—discipline will move you forward, but self-compassion will keep you grounded. With patience, persistence, and adaptability, you'll create habits that not only stick but also bring lasting fulfillment and growth to your life.

Chapter 8:
The Reset and Rise Habit Plan

We are what we repeatedly do. –Aristotle

Resetting your habits and rising to your full potential isn't just about ambition—it's about transforming intentions into actions. It's about consciously shifting your behaviors, mindset, and routines to align with the person you aspire to become. Imagine your routines as the foundation of a sturdy bridge, connecting where you are now to where you dream of being. Each small, consistent step forward strengthens that structure, moving you one step closer to your ideal future. The power of those tiny actions compounds over time, like the building blocks of a strong, resilient bridge that can withstand both calm days and stormy weather.

Think of it like this: every habit you form is a deliberate investment in yourself. Whether you're balancing a demanding career, rebuilding after setbacks, or deepening connections with loved ones, your habits shape your journey. They are the key to unlocking the potential that lies dormant within you. By taking control of your habits, you're not simply checking off tasks or achieving fleeting goals. You're building a future that reflects your true values—one where you are fully aligned with your purpose.

This process isn't just about success—it's about achieving lasting balance across all areas of your life. It's about recognizing that even the most monumental shifts begin with the small, daily choices you make. Whether it's finding time for personal growth amidst a busy schedule, maintaining a consistent workout routine to improve your health, or committing to daily reflection to foster inner peace, each of these actions, no matter how small, contributes to a larger, meaningful transformation.

When you start to rewire your habits—slowly and deliberately—you begin to see not just the changes you can make today but the lifelong results you can achieve. In this chapter, we'll explore the steps to reset your habits, take practical, intentional actions that align with your deepest desires, and create a life that feels both fulfilling and balanced. Your habits are the bridge between where you are now and where you dream to be, and each step you take builds the path toward your most empowered and authentic self.

Crafting Your Personalized Habit Roadmap

Designing a personalized habit plan involves outlining purposeful actions and routines that will lead to fulfillment and productivity. It all starts with crafting a clear vision of what success looks like for you—a guiding star to navigate the terrain of your aspirations and daily challenges.

The first step in developing this plan is vision clarification. Imagine where you want to be in the future, in your personal and professional life. Your vision serves as a motivational compass, guiding you toward your goals even amid distractions or setbacks. For instance, if your vision is to maintain a balanced lifestyle that prioritizes health and work productivity, every habit you adopt should reflect this picture of success.

By clarifying your vision, you tap into a source of motivation that propels you forward and cultivates resilience in the face of obstacles. Below is a worksheet designed to help you craft a personalized habit plan that aligns with your unique goals and aspirations.

Goal-Setting Worksheet: Define and Celebrate Progress

Step 1: Define Your Goal

Define your main goal in clear, specific terms.

Main goal: _____

Why is this goal important to you? Identify the core values or personal motivations behind this goal.

My "Why": _____

What does success look like? Describe what accomplishing this goal would look or feel like.

Success looks like:
_____

List the smaller, actionable tasks that will help you achieve this goal.

_____
_____
_____
_____
_____
_____

Step 2: Weekly Progress Tracker

Week	Small goal	Completed Yes or No	Notes	Celebration plan
1				
2				
3				
4				

Daily Check-In

Use this tracker to monitor your efforts each day.

Day	Task: Completed Yes or No	Notes
Monday		
Tuesday		
Wednesday		
Thursday		
Friday		
Saturday		
Sunday		

Step 3: Celebrate Small Wins

What small wins have you achieved so far? Write down any milestones or progress you've made, no matter how minor.

Small win 1: _____

Small win 2: _____

Small win 3: _____

How will you celebrate? Choose rewards that align with your goal or bring you joy.

Examples of small celebrations:

Treat yourself to a favorite snack or meal.

Take a relaxing break (for example, a long bath or a nature walk).

Share your success with a friend or mentor.

Reward plan 1: _____

Reward plan 2: _____

Reward plan 3: _____

Step 4: Reflect and Adjust

What's working? Identify strategies or habits that have helped you make progress.

Helpful strategies:
_____

What needs improvement? Identify any obstacles or habits that are slowing you down.

Areas for improvement: _____

What adjustments will you make moving forward? Modify your approach to stay on track.

Adjustments: _____

Step 5: Long-Term Vision

Looking back, what have you learned from this process? Reflect on insights gained while working toward your goal.

Lessons learned: _____

What's your next goal? Use the momentum you've built to tackle another challenge or dream.

Next goal: _____

Implementing Your Plan

Incorporating a timeline into your habit plan fosters accountability and helps track progress. Setting specific deadlines for implementing, evaluating, and adjusting habits helps you stay on course without feeling rushed. These deadlines act as checkpoints, allowing you to reflect on your progress and make necessary modifications. For instance, you might discover that exercising in the morning boosts your energy for the day, or you may realize that tweaking your evening routine helps you wind down more effectively. These insights allow you to optimize your habits in real time, ensuring they align with your goals.

Additionally, use tools such as habit-tracking apps, journals, or planners to monitor your progress and celebrate small victories. These tools serve as visual reminders of your commitment, helping you stay focused and providing tangible proof of your efforts. Together, these strategies strengthen your plan, making your journey toward lasting change both effective and rewarding.

As you move forward, remember that your habit plan isn't set in stone—it's a flexible guide that grows with you. Take time to pause and reflect regularly on what's working and what's not. Maybe you notice that some habits no longer serve you, or perhaps you find new approaches that make your routine more effective. Adjusting your plan along the way keeps it relevant and ensures it continues to support your goals. Think of it as a living framework that evolves as your needs and priorities change.

What makes a personalized habit plan so powerful is its ability to fit seamlessly into different phases of life. Whether you're navigating a busy career, recovering from a setback, or balancing the demands of parenting, your plan can adapt to suit your unique circumstances. It's not rigid, and you can tweak it at any time, helping you create sustainable, meaningful change over time. By keeping it flexible and aligned with your vision, you set yourself up for growth and a fulfilling life.

Setting and Celebrating Milestones

When it comes to personal growth, breaking goals into manageable milestones prevents overwhelm and ensures steady progress. It's how you stay motivated and keep track of your progress without feeling like you're drowning in the big picture. Think of milestones as little checkpoints on your way to achieving those big dreams. They help you focus, keep you organized, and make everything feel way less overwhelming. Here's the thing—when you take a massive goal and break it into smaller, doable steps, you're setting yourself up for success. This approach is essential for staying on track and keeping your momentum. It's like having signposts along a twisty road: each one brings you closer to your destination, and hitting those checkpoints feels like a mini victory every time. For example, let's say you want to get fitter. Instead of vaguely saying, "I want to be healthier," you could aim for specific, measurable goals, like finishing three workouts a week or hitting small weight-loss milestones. Each time you reach one, you'll feel that sense of accomplishment, which keeps you pumped to keep going.

Create a Balance Between Short-Term Wins and Long-Term Goals

Balancing short-term achievements with long-term goals is another key aspect. While it's natural to dream big, focusing solely on the endgame can lead to burnout or loss of interest. Instead, try incorporating immediate wins to help you stay motivated. For instance, if you want to publish your novel, the entire process might feel overwhelming. But if you break it into milestones—like writing a certain number of words daily or finishing one chapter at a time—it makes the journey feel manageable. Additionally, every time they tick off a milestone, you get that boost of motivation to keep going. It's all about celebrating those little wins while keeping your eye on the bigger prize. That balance is what keeps you energized and moving forward.

Celebrate Your Accomplishments

Celebrating your wins—big or small—is such an important part of building new habits. Taking time to recognize your progress keeps you motivated and makes the whole process more enjoyable. And here's the good news: celebrations don't have to be anything fancy. A small treat, like your favorite meal, a relaxing day off, or even just taking a moment to acknowledge your hard work, can do wonders for your mindset. Writing down your goals and tracking your progress creates a positive feedback loop that keeps you engaged and excited to keep going.

Remain Adaptable

As you pursue your milestones, staying adaptable is crucial. Life is unpredictable, and rigidly sticking to your set goals without considering changing circumstances can lead to frustration or, worse—failure. Being flexible with your milestones allows you to make the necessary adjustments in response to challenges or new insights. Let's say you've set a milestone to finish a project on a specific date, but unexpected events disrupt your timeline. Adapting your plan to accommodate these changes—without abandoning your ultimate goal—ensures you stick to the plan until you achieve your goal. This flexibility might involve adjusting deadlines, redefining your tasks, or even altering the milestones. Adaptability reinforces resilience and teaches you to deal with setbacks gracefully, turning challenges into opportunities for growth.

If you're balancing a hectic schedule, creating manageable milestones enables you to integrate new habits seamlessly into your routine. By focusing on small, actionable steps, you can establish healthier practices without getting overwhelmed. Similarly, if you're recovering from a setback, flexible milestones provide a way to regain control, rebuild confidence, and move forward with purpose—one step at a time.

And if you're juggling parenthood, breaking goals into manageable chunks can help you balance personal growth with family responsibilities. For example, if your goal is to spend more quality time with your kids or prioritize self-care, setting small, achievable milestones ensures that you make progress without feeling like you have to sacrifice one priority for another. It's all about finding a rhythm that works for you and celebrating every little step along the way.

Setting guidelines can make this journey even smoother. When balancing short-term and long-term milestones, it's key to approach them practically. Start by identifying what you want to achieve in the near future—like specific skills or experiences—and make sure these align with your bigger, long-term goals. Since life rarely unfolds in a straight line, it's important to regularly revisit and adjust your goals to stay in tune with your evolving priorities and interests. Flexibility is the secret to staying on track, even when life throws unexpected twists your way.

When it comes to celebrating milestones, create rituals that feel personal and meaningful. Maybe it's taking a moment to reflect on your progress, treating yourself to something special, or sharing the joy with friends and family. These simple acts turn achievements into memorable moments that keep you motivated. And don't forget to stay open to change. Regularly check in with your strategies and don't hesitate to tweak or redefine your milestones as needed. This mindset keeps you moving forward, encourages growth, and ensures you're always learning and improving.

Tracking Progress and Reflecting on Habits

Tracking and reflecting are vital to building lasting habits and celebrating progress. With the right tools and techniques, you can make steady progress toward your goals while enjoying a sense of accomplishment along the way.

Let's start with tracking methods. It's essential to have a system that suits your schedule and preferences.

Practice Journaling

Journaling is a timeless and effective tool for tracking habits, reflecting on experiences, and celebrating progress. Writing things down each day creates a routine that encourages mindfulness and builds accountability. It's not just about logging habits—it's also a therapeutic way to process your thoughts and emotions. Journals encourage self-reflection, helping you acknowledge challenges, celebrate wins, and track growth as it happens.

Use Digital Apps

If you prefer a more tech-savvy approach, habit-tracking apps are a fantastic option. These apps offer an organized, efficient way to monitor habits and set reminders, making them ideal for busy lifestyles. Many apps include customizable notifications to keep you on track, along with visual progress reports that show your growth at a glance. Seeing your progress in charts or graphs can be incredibly motivating—it turns abstract goals into tangible results. Some apps even include community features, allowing you to share milestones and insights with others. This adds an element of social connection, boosting your motivation through shared experiences.

Reflect Regularly

Tracking habits is a great first step, but reflection is where the real magic happens. It's through reflection that raw data becomes meaningful insight. Regular check-ins guided by thoughtful questions can serve as crucial milestones in your habit journey. Consider asking yourself:

What went well this week?

What challenges did I face?

How did I adapt to overcome them?

These questions encourage self-awareness, helping you evaluate what's working and identify areas for improvement.

Reflection should always be balanced—celebrate your successes, no matter how small, but also use setbacks as opportunities to grow. Recognizing your wins reinforces positive habits, while constructive critiques allow you to make adjustments where needed.

Reflection isn't just about looking back; it's also about planning ahead. By regularly assessing your progress, you can fine-tune your strategies and adapt them to align with your evolving goals. This proactive approach ensures that your habits remain meaningful and effective, no matter how life changes.

Celebrate Success and Learn From Setbacks

Celebrating your achievements is a powerful way to stay motivated and reinforce new habits. The key is to make it personal. Choose rewards that genuinely resonate with you and fit your lifestyle. It could be something simple, like treating yourself to your favorite dessert, enjoying a relaxing spa day, or even writing yourself a heartfelt note of congratulations. The goal is to associate your accomplishments with joy and fulfillment, creating a positive feedback loop that strengthens your intrinsic motivation over time.

Harness the Power of Community

Engaging with a supportive community can take your tracking and reflection efforts to the next level. Sharing your successes with others—whether it's in online forums, local groups, or among close friends not only creates a sense of accountability but also provides external validation. Knowing that others are aware of your goals acts as an extra motivator to stay on track. These communities don't just celebrate your wins—they also encourage collective growth. You get to exchange advice, share experiences, and offer encouragement, making the journey more rewarding and less lonely. Discussing your victories and challenges in these spaces can turn individual progress into a shared learning experience.

Being part of a community isn't just about celebrating success—it's also about having a safe space to share setbacks and struggles. Openly discussing your challenges can lead to tailored advice, fresh perspectives, and practical solutions you might not have considered on your own. Receiving support through the highs and lows builds resilience and increases your chances of sticking to your habits. With the right balance of personal rewards and community support, you can turn every step of your journey—big or small—into an opportunity for growth and celebration.

Building Your Roadmap to Lasting Growth

As we conclude this chapter, remember that building a personalized habit plan is more than just a framework—it's an intentional commitment to your growth. Your journey begins with clarity, anchored by your vision, and gains momentum through focused habits and actionable steps. By keeping your approach flexible and open to change, you can handle life's challenges while staying aligned with your goals.

Remember, your journey is uniquely yours, and the beauty of this approach lies in its flexibility to fit your current life circumstances. Celebrate your wins, no matter how small, because each step forward is proof of your progress. Reflect often, adjust as needed, and lean on the strength of the community for encouragement and shared wisdom. This process isn't about perfection; it's about persistence and the power of small, consistent actions to create lasting change.

As you move forward, trust that your habit plan is more than a tool; it's a pathway to a life of purpose, growth, and fulfillment. With dedication and adaptability, the future you envision will gradually unfold, one intentional habit at a time.

Chapter 9:

Routines That Elevate

Sow a thought, reap an action; sow an action, reap a habit; sow a habit, reap a character; sow a character, reap a destiny. –Stephen R. Covey

Imagine waking up, the weight of yesterday's chaos still lingering in your mind. Your to-do list is long, your energy is low, and the thought of tackling everything feels overwhelming. But what if, instead of diving straight into the demands of the day, you took a moment to pause? What if, for just a few minutes, you could ground yourself in a routine that sets the tone for the rest of your day?

Think about it: a few months ago, you might have felt trapped in a cycle of stress and exhaustion. Juggling your career, family life, and personal goals might have left you feeling like you were constantly running behind. Every day might have seemed like a race to get through without ever taking a breath. But imagine deciding to try something different. Consider carving out 15 minutes each morning just for yourself. No emails, no phone calls, no rushing to the next task. Instead, you could focus on something simple—like drinking a warm cup of tea while journaling your intentions for the day.

At first, it might seem like a small, insignificant change. But over time, those 15 minutes could become your anchor. They would give you the chance to reflect on your values and priorities, helping you realign your actions with what truly matters. Slowly, you'll notice how this small habit could transform the way you approach your day. Instead of reacting to the chaos, you start to feel more in control. Your energy balances out, and you feel more focused. Those quiet moments of reflection give you the clarity you need to move through your day with intention and purpose.

This could be your story: elevating your routines isn't about perfection or checking off every item on your list. It's about creating space for meaningful growth, even in the smallest of actions. What if every day held the potential for balance and growth? By starting with intentional habits, you could shift the course of your day—and, ultimately, your life. You have the ability to turn chaos into clarity, burnout into balance, and ordinary days into something extraordinary.

Creating Empowering Routines

Structured routines are one of the most powerful tools for building personal development and creating habits that last. By crafting intentional practices around key parts of your day—morning, afternoon, evening, and even weekends—you can create a rhythm that supports productivity, mental clarity, and overall well-being.

Morning Routine

A morning routine is your launchpad for the day, providing structure and setting a positive tone. Think of it as your personal ritual for creating momentum. Mindfulness practices, like meditation or deep breathing, clear mental clutter and help center your thoughts before the day begins.

This moment of calmness helps you focus on the present, creating a peaceful mindset that influences how you approach the rest of your day.

Incorporating physical activity is key to jumpstarting your body and mind. Whether it's a quick jog around the block, a few yoga stretches, or a set of simple stretches, moving your body helps increase blood flow, release endorphins, and boost energy levels. Exercise in the morning also improves focus and sharpens your mind, giving you the mental clarity needed to tackle challenges.

Together, these elements of your morning routine prepare you to face the day with increased vitality, positivity, and clarity. Rather than waking up and rushing into tasks, you've set a clear, intentional tone that helps you start your day on the right foot, which carries over into your work, relationships, and well-being throughout the day.

Afternoon Routine

By the time afternoon rolls around, you may start to notice a dip in your energy and focus. This is completely normal, but it's important to have a strategy in place to keep yourself motivated and productive. To combat afternoon fatigue, take short, intentional breaks each hour—brief walks, stretches, or deep breathing exercises to reset your mind.

During these breaks, consider adding a simple gratitude practice. Taking a moment to jot down three things you're thankful for can shift your focus away from stress or frustration and cultivate a more positive outlook. It's easy to get caught up in what's going wrong, but actively choosing to reflect on the positive can reframe your mindset and help you stay grounded.

Another effective strategy to maintain momentum in the afternoon is using focused work sessions, such as the Pomodoro Technique. This method breaks your work at intervals—typically 25 minutes of focused work followed by a 5-minute break. This approach helps prevent burnout by balancing intense focus with brief periods of rest, ensuring that you remain productive without feeling overwhelmed. The combination of purposeful breaks, gratitude exercises, and structured work intervals will help you stay energized, focused, and motivated throughout the afternoon.

Evening Routine

An evening routine is essential for helping you transition from the busyness of the day to a restful and rejuvenating night. This shift from productivity to rest is important for maintaining a healthy balance between action and relaxation. The evening is your time to unwind and reflect, preparing both your body and mind for a good night's sleep, which is crucial for overall well-being.

Start by creating a calming environment that signals to your body that it's time to wind down. Dimming the lights or using soft lighting helps lower the level of stimulation and signals to your brain that the day is coming to an end. This reduction in bright light cues your body to start producing melatonin, the hormone responsible for making you feel sleepy.

Research suggests maintaining a room temperature between 60 and 67°F (15–19°C) promotes restful sleep (Green, 2022). This simple adjustment can improve the depth and quality of your sleep, helping you wake up feeling refreshed.

Disconnecting from screens is another important aspect of your evening routine. The blue light emitted by phones, computers, and televisions can interfere with the production of melatonin, making it harder for you to fall asleep. Aim to stop using electronic devices at least 30 minutes to an hour before bed, giving your mind time to disengage from digital stimuli and relax.

One of the most beneficial practices to incorporate into your evening routine is journaling. Writing in a journal before bed allows you to reflect on your day in a meaningful way. Take a moment to celebrate the wins—whether big or small—that you experienced throughout the day. This helps create a sense of accomplishment and positive closure. At the same time, journaling gives you the opportunity to process any challenges you face, allowing you to release any stress or frustration before bed. Additionally, planning for tomorrow—whether it's setting intentions or outlining your tasks—can help you feel organized and less anxious as you close out the day.

Incorporating these calming practices into your evening routine not only improves sleep quality but also nurtures a sense of peace and mindfulness. This peaceful end to your day helps you let go of the tensions of the day and prepares your body and mind for restorative sleep, enabling you to wake up ready to face tomorrow with energy and clarity.

Weekend Routine

The weekend presents a unique opportunity to step back, recharge, and prepare for the week ahead. While it's important to allow yourself some rest and relaxation, having a structured weekend routine can help you set a strong foundation for the coming days, ensuring that you feel organized, energized, and ready to tackle your goals with clarity and focus.

One of the key benefits of a weekend routine is the time it gives you to reflect and plan. Use part of your weekend to assess how the past week went, both in terms of your accomplishments and areas that could use improvement. Celebrating the progress you've made reinforces positive habits and keeps you motivated while also giving you an opportunity to acknowledge your successes. Reflecting on any setbacks or challenges allows you to learn from them and adjust your strategies for the upcoming week.

Meal prepping is a perfect example of how a weekend routine can set you up for success. Taking the time to prepare meals in advance not only saves time during busy weekdays, but also encourages healthier eating habits. When you plan and prep meals, you eliminate the stress of last-minute decisions about what to eat, and you're more likely to make nourishing choices instead of opting for unhealthy fast food or snacks. This simple act of planning ahead can have a big impact on both your energy levels and overall well-being throughout the week.

Additionally, use your weekend to review and organize your schedule for the upcoming week. Take a close look at your commitments, appointments, and deadlines, and make adjustments as needed. Anticipating potential challenges—whether it's a busy workday or family obligations—allows you to plan ahead and manage your time more effectively. If you foresee any obstacles, having a backup plan can help alleviate stress and keep you on track.

Weekends are also a great time to set intentions for the week ahead. Whether it's personal, professional, or health-related, setting specific goals for the coming week ensures that you stay focused and motivated. Take a moment to visualize what you want to achieve and break those goals down into actionable steps. This will give you a clear roadmap for the week, making it easier to stay on track and feel a sense of accomplishment as you move forward.

Incorporating structured routines into your weekend creates a balanced rhythm that supports your ongoing personal development and goal-setting. Whether you're kickstarting your mornings with mindfulness, recharging in the afternoons with rest, unwinding in the evenings with a calming ritual, or setting yourself up for the week ahead, these intentional practices keep you grounded, organized, and energized. By using the weekend wisely, you set yourself up for smoother, more productive weekdays and ensure that your personal growth journey remains steady and focused.

Designing Personalized Morning and Evening Rituals

Creating personalized morning and evening rituals is a powerful way to align your daily routine with your personal goals. To start this process, it's important to identify individual preferences that allow you to tailor your rituals according to your unique lifestyle. Understanding what triggers stress or joy in your life can help you create practices that truly resonate with you, leading to more consistency and fulfillment. Flexibility is key here; some days, you may feel the need for a vigorous morning exercise session, while on other days, a few minutes of meditation may be all you need. The essence of these rituals is adaptability to suit your changing needs.

Morning Rituals

Effective morning rituals often include a combination of gratitude, physical exercise, and goal setting. These three elements work together to create a proactive mindset for the day ahead. Starting your morning with gratitude shifts your focus toward positivity, increasing your resilience to challenges. Physical exercise, whether it's a short yoga practice or a brisk walk, boosts your energy and focus, setting the tone for a productive day. Goal setting offers clarity and direction, reducing aimlessness and increasing productivity. As Robin Sharma suggests in The 5 A.M. Club, waking up early, and dedicating time to fitness, reflection, and learning can put you in a flow state conducive to success (Sharma, 2019).

Evening Rituals

Evening rituals, in contrast, focus on winding down and preparing your mind and body for rest. Reflection plays a key role here, helping you assess what went well during the day and identify areas for improvement. Relaxation techniques, such as deep breathing or reading, can significantly reduce tension and anxiety, ensuring you transition smoothly into a restful sleep. Additionally, planning for the next day can help reduce morning anxiety, providing a clear sense of purpose as you wake up.

As you refine your routines, it's essential to stay flexible and open to changes. What worked at the beginning of your journey may need adjustments as your circumstances evolve. Regular reflection on your rituals will help you identify when they no longer serve your needs or goals. For example, if a high-intensity morning workout becomes too exhausting, swapping it for a gentler practice may better suit your current energy levels.

By embracing personal preferences, incorporating effective components, planning thoughtfully, and adapting when necessary, these rituals become the foundation of your habit-building journey. Creating a realistic timeframe is also essential for maintaining these practices without feeling overwhelmed. This balance ensures that your rituals not only fit seamlessly into your daily life but also help you stay on track toward achieving your personal goals.

Weekly Preparations for Success

Setting up a successful week begins with thoughtful preparation and strategic planning. By creating routines that anchor your daily activities, you can bring structure to your days, making life more organized and less overwhelming. With a few strategic practices, your week can turn into a well-balanced and purpose-driven experience.

Weekly Review Sessions

Regular review sessions are a powerful habit for reflection and growth. Taking time at the end of each week to assess what went well and areas of improvement sets the stage for growth. These sessions provide an opportunity to celebrate your achievements, identify challenges, and fine-tune strategies for the week ahead. A simple practice, like journaling your weekly highlights and struggles, can encourage continuous learning while helping you stay motivated by recognizing even the smallest wins.

These reviews also help uncover patterns or recurring challenges that may otherwise go unnoticed. For example, you might realize that certain tasks consistently take longer than planned or that your energy peaks at specific times of the day. By identifying these trends, you can proactively adjust your schedule to align with your strengths and limitations. Embrace these moments of reflection as opportunities to refine your priorities and keep building momentum toward your goals.

Time Blocking for Priorities

Time blocking is an effective technique to manage your responsibilities while maximizing focus and productivity. By dedicating specific time slots to individual tasks, you can better visualize your day and distribute your energy more intentionally. Start by listing all your weekly tasks, then sort them based on urgency and importance. Assign specific blocks of time in your calendar to tackle these tasks according to their priority. Don't forget to include buffer periods between activities to account for unexpected interruptions and avoid over-scheduling yourself.

This not only creates a structured workflow, but also promotes deeper concentration. Knowing exactly what you need to do and when enables you to focus on the task at hand without distraction. For example, setting aside Monday mornings for brainstorming or creative work ensures you can fully engage without worrying about other responsibilities. Time blocking helps you establish a disciplined approach where you give each task the attention it deserves, optimizing your efficiency and reducing stress.

Meal and Nutrition Plans

Healthy eating is essential for maintaining energy and overall well-being, and planning your meals in advance can simplify daily decision-making. By developing meal and nutrition plans, you can establish mindful eating habits that align with your lifestyle and dietary goals. Set aside time during the weekend to plan menus, batch, cook, and prepare ingredients for the week ahead. Creating a grocery list based on your plan not only saves time but also ensures healthy choices are convenient and accessible.

When your meals are pre-planned, you're less likely to resort to unhealthy fast food options due to time constraints. Having nutritious meals readily available supports steady energy levels throughout the week. Cooking food in batches not only saves time but also encourages portion control, which can help you maintain a balanced diet. As you implement these nutrition strategies, you'll find yourself more in tune with your body's needs, helping you sustain a healthier lifestyle.

Scheduling Self-Care Activities

Making self-care a non-negotiable part of your schedule is critical for maintaining balance and building resilience. By intentionally setting aside time for personal well-being, you prioritize rest and recovery, which are essential for long-term productivity and mental clarity. Incorporate activities that nurture your mind, body, and spirit into your weekly routine. Whether it's dedicating time to physical exercise, hobbies, meditation, or simply relaxing with a good book, these moments of self-care promote a healthier, more balanced lifestyle. Scheduling self-care prevents burnout, ensuring you have the energy and focus to meet life's demands.

Prioritizing self-care not only benefits you, but also sets a powerful example for others. It reinforces the idea that well-being is foundational to success in all areas of life. By intentionally carving out time to recharge, you'll find yourself better equipped to handle both personal and professional challenges with renewed energy and perspective.

Below is a checklist to help you create routines that align with your goals.

Checklist: Creating Routines That Align With Your Personal and Professional Goals

Clarify your goals

Define your personal and professional priorities.

Identify your long-term vision and key objectives.

Break larger goals into smaller, actionable steps.

Assess your current habits

List your daily routines and time-consuming activities.

Identify habits that support or hinder your goals.

Highlight gaps where new routines are needed.

Set intentional habits

Choose two to three habits that directly align with your goals.

Ensure they are specific, measurable, and realistic.

Focus on habits that create the most significant impact.

Design your daily schedule

Assign time blocks for each habit or routine.

Include buffer time for unexpected changes.

Start small and gradually build consistency.

Reflect and adjust

Regularly assess whether your routines align with your goals.

Ask yourself: Are these habits working for me? What needs to change?

Adapt as needed based on new insights or circumstances.

Prioritize self-care

Include habits that support your physical, mental, and emotional well-being.

Schedule downtime and moments of rest to avoid burnout.

Balance work and personal growth for overall harmony.

Commit and stay consistent

Remind yourself of the "why" behind your goals.

Focus on showing up, even on less-than-perfect days.

Trust the process and celebrate your evolution over time.

The Power of Intentional Routines

Intentional habits are key to dealing with daily challenges. Whether it's starting the day with positivity, maintaining focus through afternoon strategies, or winding down with calming evening practices, these routines help you align your actions with your aspirations.

Remember, these habits aren't about perfection but progress—a continual commitment to creating a life that reflects your goals and values. As you implement these strategies, you're taking an active role in shaping your days into meaningful experiences.

As we come to the end of this book, the journey doesn't end here. Every small step you take in adopting these habits brings you closer to a life of ongoing growth, resilience, and joy. As you move forward, let these routines become a source of strength and a reflection of the life you're creating.

Conclusion

It's not what we do once in a while that shapes our lives. It's what we do consistently. —Tony Robbins

In the chaos of daily life, it's easy to overlook the gift each day offers: a blank slate, ready for a fresh start. Like nature's seasons renewing the earth, every morning carries the promise of change. This simple truth reminds us that we can reshape our habits, thoughts, and perspectives— not through dramatic overnight changes, but through consistent, intentional actions.

Imagine waking up each day with the quiet whisper of possibility nudging you forward. It's not about tackling everything at once but about taking small, purposeful steps that build meaningful change over time. These daily opportunities to reset help turn even the most intimidating goals into achievable milestones. The key lies in setting goals that matter deeply to you.

In today's world, which glorifies trends and instant gratification, defining your "why" anchors you to something real. Think about the difference between pursuing a goal because it sounds impressive and pursuing it because it carries personal significance. Are you training for a marathon to check it off your bucket list, or is it about reclaiming your health, pushing past old limits, or proving something to yourself? Understanding your "why" provides clarity, fuels motivation, and keeps you grounded when challenges arise. When your actions are tied to meaningful intentions, you build habits aligned with your values, fostering resilience to overcome setbacks and avoid distractions while staying connected to your purpose.

Progress isn't just about the finish line—it's about celebrating the small wins along the way. Each small victory, no matter how minor, sparks motivation. Whether it's crossing off one task on your to-do list or celebrating a moment of discipline, these tiny triumphs build momentum. Over time, they stack up, carrying you forward and making even the most challenging goals feel within reach.

Our lives are built upon small achievements, each one laying the foundation for a larger purpose. Recognizing these small victories fuels momentum, much like a snowball gathering size and strength as it rolls downhill. These seemingly small successes create the energy and confidence needed to continue moving forward.

However, no journey is without challenges. You will encounter setbacks and obstacles that test your commitment. Instead of viewing these challenges as insurmountable barriers, see them as valuable learning experiences. Picture the tightrope walker—when they stumble, they pause, regain their balance, and adjust before carrying on. Every setback offers a chance to reassess strategies and grow stronger, building resilience along the way.

True resilience comes from embracing imperfection. Progress—not perfection—is the ultimate goal. Every stumble offers insights into what works and what doesn't, guiding you toward sustainable improvement. This mindset shift allows you to approach challenges with patience and a focus on learning rather than on harsh self-judgment.

Creating lasting change is not a sprint but a marathon. Nurturing healthy habits amid life's demands requires consistency, patience, and the willingness to celebrate small wins. Progress builds slowly, but when combined with intentionality and resilience, it leads to a meaningful, lasting transformation that integrates seamlessly into all aspects of life.

If you're juggling a demanding schedule, achieving a work-life balance may feel elusive. Yet, as we've explored, success lies in small resets, intentional goals, and steady progress. By celebrating milestones and approaching hurdles with patience, you can create a life where personal well-being and professional success coexist. Or perhaps you're going through a significant life transition—whether recovery, reinvention, or redirection—you can find strength in this process. By focusing on intentional actions, appreciating each step forward, and recognizing the lessons within setbacks, you create space for growth, renewal, and a deeper connection to your journey.

Ultimately, the path to healthier habits and purposeful living is deeply personal. Each path is unique, yet the principles remain the same: choose to begin again, celebrate progress, and embrace challenges as part of the process. With patience, intention, and unwavering resolve, every step you take brings you closer to the life you envision. Remember, transformation is not an endpoint but a continuous process of growth and discovery. So, embrace the blank slate each day brings. Celebrate small steps, connect with your purpose, and trust that real, lasting change comes from showing up consistently—one intentional moment at a time.

Appendix A

Habit Formation Template

Habit: _____

Week of: _____

Weekly Tracker

Day	Completed	Time spent	Reflections
Monday			
Tuesday			
Wednesday			
Thursday			
Friday			
Saturday			
Sunday			

Reflections

Biggest win of the week:
_____

Challenges of the week:
_____

Strategy for improvement:
_____

Measuring Progress

Progress toward achieving goal: Poor/okay/great/outstanding

Motivation rating (1-10): _____

Monthly Habit Tracker

Habit name: _____

Month: _____

Sun	Mon	Tue	Wed	Thurs	Fri	Sat
1	2	3	4	5	6	7
8	9	10	11	12	13	14
15	16	17	18	19	20	21
22	23	24	25	26	27	28
29	30	31				

Appendix B

Habit Loop Breakdown

Instructions

Identify a habit you want to build, change, or break. Break it into its three core components: cue (trigger), routine (action), and reward (outcome), and reflect on ways to adjust the loop.

Step 1: Identify the Habit

What habit do you want to analyze? (for example, snacking on junk food, skipping workouts, procrastinating)

Write it here:

_____
_____

Step 2: Define the Habit Loop

Cue (Trigger): What triggers the habit?

time of day?

location?

emotional state (boredom, stress)?

people around you?

an event or specific action?

Examples:

"When I feel stressed at work (emotional state)."

"Every afternoon at 3 p.m. (time of day)."

Write your cue or trigger:

_____

_____

Routine (Action): What action do you take in response to the cue? (Be specific.)

Example: "I grab a sugary snack from the kitchen."

Write the routine or action:

_____

_____

Reward (Outcome): What reward do you get from the habit?

relief?

satisfaction?

comfort?

energy boost?

example: "I feel a momentary energy boost and relief from stress."

Write the reward or outcome:

_____

_____

Step 3: Reflect and Adjust the Habit Loop

Understand the reward: Is there another way to achieve this reward with a healthier habit?

For example, if snacking gives you stress relief, could deep breathing, stretching, or a quick walk offer the same outcome?

Alternative actions that provide the same reward:

_____
_____

Replace the routine: What healthier or more productive routine can you swap into the loop?

Replace the old action with a new one that fulfills the same need.

New routine to try:

_____
_____

Plan for the cue: What steps can you take to avoid or manage the trigger?

Can you change your environment?

Set reminders?

Prepare for the cue ahead of time?

Plan to address the cue/trigger:

_____
_____

Step 4: Create a Habit Action Plan

Write your new habit loop

Cue: _____

New routine:

_____

Reward: _____

Identify obstacles

What challenges might make this habit difficult to stick to?

Accountability plan

how will you track progress?

habit tracker, journal, or app?

weekly check-in with a friend or mentor?

Your tracking method:

_____

_____

Start small and celebrate wins

What small steps will you take to build this habit?

Example: "Exercise for just 5 minutes a day."

Write your small steps:

_____

_____

How will you celebrate small successes?

_____

_____

Reflection question:

At the end of the week, ask yourself: What worked well? What needs adjustment?

_____

_____

Final note: Consistency and patience are key. By identifying the cues, adjusting routines, and focusing on rewards, you can gradually create lasting, positive habits.

Daily Habit Tracker

Habit name:
_____

Week:
_____

Day of the week	Morning	Afternoon	Evening	Notes
Monday	Example: 1 glass while prepping coffee or tea.	2 glasses with light snacks.	1 glass while watching TV.	Feeling more energetic today.
Tuesday				
Wednesday				
Thursday				
Friday				
Saturday				
Sunday				

Streak Tracker

Habit name: _____

Month: _____

Day	Completed?	Longest streak	Current streak
Day 1			
Day 2			
Day 3			
Day 30/31			

Appendix C

Resource List for Developing New Habits and Resetting Your Life

Here's a curated list of resources to help you continue growing, building new habits, and embracing meaningful change in your life.

Books

Atomic Habits by James Clear Learn how tiny changes can lead to remarkable results. This book is packed with practical strategies for habit formation and breaking negative patterns.

The Power of Habit by Charles Duhigg An exploration of how habits work and how to transform them for personal and professional success.

Essentialism: The Disciplined Pursuit of Less by Greg McKeown A guide to focusing on what truly matters by eliminating unnecessary distractions.

Grit: The Power of Passion and Perseverance by Angela Duckworth Learn about the importance of persistence and passion in achieving long-term goals.

Mindset: The New Psychology of Success by Carol S. Dweck Discover how adopting a growth mindset can help you overcome setbacks and embrace lifelong learning.

Apps

Habitica: Turn habit formation into a fun, gamified experience. Earn rewards for completing tasks and track your progress in a unique RPG-style interface.

Streaks: A user-friendly app designed to help you create and maintain daily habits through streak tracking.

Insight timer: A meditation and mindfulness app with thousands of free guided meditations, perfect for developing focus and reducing stress.

Forest: Stay productive and cultivate focus by planting virtual trees as you work toward completing tasks or breaking habits like procrastination.

Trello: A task management tool that helps you visually organize goals, projects, and habits to stay on track.

Podcasts

The Habit Coach by Ashdin doctor: Bite-sized episodes that offer actionable advice on creating positive habits and improving daily routines.

The James Flear podcast: Hosted by the author of *Atomic Habits*, this podcast explores the science of habits and self-improvement.

The Minimalists podcast: Focuses on simplifying your life and eliminating habits or possessions that no longer serve you.

How to Fail with Elizabeth day: Inspirational interviews that explore how failure can be a catalyst for growth and habit transformation.

Optimal Living Daily: Daily readings of personal development articles covering productivity, mindfulness, and healthy living.

Online Courses

"Tiny Habits" with BJ Fogg (via Udemy or his website). A practical course on starting small and building life-changing habits.

Master class: "Designing Your Life" by Bill Burnett and Dave Evans. Learn how to use design thinking to create the life you want, including insights into habit development.

Coursera: The Science of Well-Being by Yale University. A free course that focuses on strategies for boosting happiness and forming healthy habits.

Other Resources

Websites and blogs

James Clear's blog: jamesclear.com

Zen Habits by Leo Babauta: zenhabits.net

Videos

TED talk: "Try Something New for 30 Days" by Matt Cutts

TED talk: "The Power of Vulnerability" by Brené Brown

These resources are designed to offer you a variety of tools and insights. Whether you're reading a transformative book, downloading an app to stay on track, or listening to a podcast for inspiration, every step you take toward resetting your habits is progress. Dive into these recommendations and find what resonates most with you!

Online Communities

Here are two excellent online communities where you can build new habits and find accountability partners:

HabitHive: This platform is designed for habit tracking and connecting with like-minded individuals. It offers features like progress tracking, habit stacking, and reflective journaling. HabitHive encourages you to pair up with accountability partners who can motivate and support you on your habit-building journey. The community aspect ensures you stay inspired and engaged while working on your personal growth goals.

Commit Club: Commit Club takes accountability a step further by incorporating challenges, including financial stakes, to keep you motivated. You can create custom challenges, pair with friends or strangers as accountability partners, and track progress through journaling. The platform allows both private and public accountability challenges, making it versatile for various goals. It also has a vibrant community area for additional inspiration and motivation.

Both communities provide unique tools and opportunities to enhance your habit-building journey, whether through structured habit tracking or innovative accountability methods.

References

Akers, A. (2023, August 3). *Preventing burnout: 7 strategies and when to seek help.* Www.medicalnewstoday.com. https://www.medicalnewstoday.com/articles/preventing-burnout

Altrogge, S. (2022, December 20). 12 morning and evening routines that will set up each day for success. *Zapier.* https://zapier.com/blog/daily-routines/

Anderson, K. (2023). Popular fad diets: An evidence-based perspective. *Progress in Cardiovascular Diseases, 77,* 78–85. https://doi.org/10.1016/j.pcad.2023.02.001

Ankor, R. (2024, February 14). *Unlocking the potential of accountability in habit formation.* Medium. https://rodeandankor.medium.com/the-power-of-accountability-harnessing-support-for-habit-success-7ee0e66c629a

Aristotle. (n.d.). *A quote by Aristotle.* The Random Vibez. Retrieved December 18, 2024, from https://www.therandomvibez.com/routine-quotes/

Aslan, A. C. (2024, August 30). *Atomic habits summary: Takeaways.* Beforesunset.ai. https://www.beforesunset.ai/post/atomic-habits-summary

Atakan, M. M., Li, Y., Koşar, Ş. N., Turnagöl, H. H., & Yan, X. (2021). Evidence-based effects of high-intensity interval training on exercise capacity and health: A review with historical perspective. *International Journal of Environmental Research and Public Health, 18*(13), 7201. https://doi.org/10.3390/ijerph18137201

Bay. (2024, May 6). *five effective strategies to overcome perfectionism.* Bay Area CBT Center. https://bayareacbtcenter.com/overcome-perfectionism/

Behavior change using gamification. (2024, February 14). Mambo Enterprise Gamification Software. https://mambo.io/gamification-guide/behaviour-change-using-gamification

The behavior hub. (2020). *The Behavior Hub.* https://www.thebehaviorhub.com/blog/2020/7/22/creating-rituals-routines-and-habits-the-how-to-of-preventative-self-care

Bell, S. (n.d.). *SMART Goals.* Mind Tools. https://www.mindtools.com/a4wo118/smart-goals

Berkman, E. T. (2018). The neuroscience of goals and behavior change. *Consulting Psychology Journal: Practice and Research, 70*(1), 28–44. https://doi.org/10.1037/cpb0000094

Beshears, J., Lee, H. N., Milkman, K. L., Mislavsky, R., & Wisdom, J. (2020). Creating exercise habits using incentives: The trade-off between flexibility and routinization. *Management Science, 67*(7). https://doi.org/10.1287/mnsc.2020.3706

Blumberg, N. (2024). Malala Yousafzai. In *Encyclopedia Britannica.* https://www.britannica.com/biography/Malala-Yousafzai

Bodell, L. (2022, December 19). *New year's resolutions fail. Do this instead.* Forbes. https://www.forbes.com/sites/lisabodell/2022/12/19/new-years-resolutions-fail-do-this-instead/

Bostick, D. (2023, December 15). *Resilience in practice: Creating a stronger self.* Anyflip.com; Darren Bostick jr. https://anyflip.com/tcpae/cymf/basic

The brighter guide to building atomic habits. (2021, July 19). Work Brighter. https://workbrighter.co/atomic-habits/

Brown, B. (2010, June). *The power of vulnerability.* Ted.com; TED Talks. https://www.ted.com/talks/brene_brown_the_power_of_vulnerability

Burnout: Signs, causes, and preventative strategies. (2024, May 7). Queen's University. https://pros.educ.queensu.ca/blog/burnout

Change your life! Change your habits! (n.d.). HabitHive. https://www.habithive.app/

Chernets, A. (2024a). How to get more done with time management worksheets. *TMetric Blog - Time Tracking Tips and Productivity Hacks.* https://blog.tmetric.com/time-management-worksheets-guide/

Chernets, A. (2024b, January 31). Top 5 time management secrets in agile methodology. *TMetric Blog - Time Tracking Tips and Productivity Hacks.* https://blog.tmetric.com/top-5-time-management-secrets-in-agile-methodology/

Clear, J. (2017, March 24). *Best podcast episodes.* James Clear. https://jamesclear.com/podcasts/episodes

Clear, J. (2018a). *Atomic habits: An easy & proven way to build good habits & break bad ones.* Penguin Publishing Group.

Clear, J. (2018b, November 13). *The 5 triggers that make new habits stick.* James Clear. https://jamesclear.com/habit-triggers

Confucius. (n.d.). *Quotes by Confucius.* A-Z Quotes. https://www.azquotes.com/quotes/topics/small-beginnings.html

Coreen, D. (2024, August 26). *The power of goal setting: An academic insight into success*in Practice. Davron. https://www.davron.net/the-power-of-goal-setting-an-academic-insight-into-success/

Covey, S. R. (n.d.). *Steven R. Covey quotes.* Gracious Quotes. https://graciousquotes.com/habit-quotes/

Cunnington, R. (2019, September 18). *Neuroplasticity: How the brain changes with learning.* IBE — Science of Learning Portal. https://solportal.ibe-unesco.org/articles/neuroplasticity-how-the-brain-changes-with-learning/

Cutts, M. (2013). *Try something new for 30 days.* TED-Ed. https://ed.ted.com/lessons/try-something-new-for-30-days-matt-cutts

Daily activity tracker app. (n.d.). Commit Club. https://commitclub.co/uses/daily-activity-tracker-app/

Defining success: A comprehensive guide to goal setting. (2024, March 22). River. https://www.riversoftware.com/leadership-development/defining-success-a-comprehensive-guide-to-goal-setting/

Design the most important project of all: your life. (n.d.). *Designing Your Life*. https://designingyour.life/

Doctor, A. (2024). *Ashdin Doctor podcast*. Ashdindoctor. https://ashdindoctor.com/ashdin-doctor-podcast-the-habit-coach/

Duckworth, A. (2018). *Grit: the power of passion and perseverance*. Collins.

Duhigg, C. (2014). *Power of habit: Why we do what we do in life and business*. Random House Trade Paperbacks. (Original work published 2012)

Dweck, C. S. (2016). *Summary of mindset : the new psychology of success*. Createspace Independent Publishing Platform.

Eckhart, M. (n.d.). *Meister Eckhart quotes*. Journey to Leadership. https://journeytoleadershipblog.com/2023/04/13/10-quotes-for-leaders-to-reset/

Effective interventions for personal growth. (n.d.). BookBaker. https://www.bookbaker.com/it/v/The-Path-to-Personal-Growth-A-Comprehensive-Guide-to-Self-Improvement-Effective-Interventions-for-Personal-Growth/8a3901e8-7059-444d-babb-e65bbe4d5218/5

Egan, P. (2021, January 16). *Creating a culture of mentorship*. Educational Renaissance. https://educationalrenaissance.com/2021/01/16/creating-a-culture-of-mentorship/

Elizabeth. (2024, October 10). *15 best accountability partner apps of 2024* . Squeeze Growth. https://squeezegrowth.com/best-accountability-partner-apps/

The evolution of Netflix: From DVDs to global streaming supremacy. (2023, June 23). Global Lancers. https://lancersglobal.com/insights/digital-transformation/the-evolution-of-netflix-from-renting-dvds-to-establishing-global-streaming-supremacy

Fogg, B. (n.d.). *Tiny Habits, Big Results: Your method for success.* Tiny Habits. https://tinyhabits.com/

Gardner, B., Lally, P., & Wardle, J. (2012). Making health habitual: the psychology of "habit-formation" and general practice. *British Journal of General Practice, 62*(605), 664–666. https://doi.org/10.3399/bjgp12x659466

Gates, B. (2015, December 7). *What you believe affects what you achieve.* Gatesnotes.com. https://www.gatesnotes.com/Mindset-The-New-Psychology-of-Success

Goal setting techniques: Ways to effectively set and achieve goals. (n.d.). Www.nsls.org. https://www.nsls.org/goal-setting-techniques

Green, E. (2022, April 16). *The best temperature for sleep.* No Sleepless Nights. https://www.nosleeplessnights.com/ideal-temperature-for-sleep/

Hardy, D. (2016). *Darren Hardy quotes.* A-Z Quotes. https://www.azquotes.com/quotes/topics/momentum.html#google_vignette

Harper, C. (n.d.). *How to build a support system for your mental health.* My Wellbeing. https://mywellbeing.com/therapy-101/how-to-build-a-support-system

Hobson, N. (2018, January 17). 4 simple habit building systems used (and perfected). *Forbes.* https://www.forbes.com/sites/nickhobson/2018/01/17/4-simple-habit-forming-systems-used-by-top-performers/

How to craft the perfect leadership development plan with tips and examples. (2023, September 1). CultureMonkey. https://www.culturemonkey.io/employee-engagement/leadership-development-plan/

How to stop sabotaging yourself and achieve success. (2024, July 15). Bay Area CBT Center. https://bayareacbtcenter.com/how-to-stop-sabotaging-yourself/

Hughes, M. (n.d.). *Personal goal setting*. Www.mindtools.com. https://www.mindtools.com/a5ykiuq/personal-goal-setting

Ian. (2024, June 5). *The 5 failures of J. K. Rowling and how she overcame them*. PressFarm. https://press.farm/5-failures-of-j-k-rowling-how-she-overcame-them/

Is an "accountability partnership" setting you up to succeed or fail? (2023, August 2). *Psychology Today*. https://www.psychologytoday.com/us/blog/the-joy-choice/202308/is-an-accountability-partnership-setting-you-up-to-succeed-or-fail

J.K. Rowling and the magic of perseverance: "I was the biggest failure I knew." (n.d.). The Literary Reporter. https://theliteraryreporter.com/j-k-rowling-and-the-magic-of-perseverance/

Johnson, G. (2016, May 10). Exercise adherence: The key to getting better client results. *The TotalCoaching Blog*. https://www.totalcoaching.com/blog/exercise-adherence/

Kays, J. L., Hurley, R. A., & Taber, K. H. (2012). The dynamic brain: Neuroplasticity and mental health. *The Journal of Neuropsychiatry and Clinical Neurosciences*, 24(2), 118–124. https://doi.org/10.1176/appi.neuropsych.12050109

Kelley, C., Lee, B., & Wilcox, L. (2017). Self-tracking for mental wellness. *Proceedings of the 2017 CHI Conference on Human Factors in Computing Systems - CHI '17*. https://doi.org/10.1145/3025453.3025750

Kmattison. (2019, September 22). *Easy weekly planning routine.* This Routine Life. https://thisroutinelife.com/weekly-planning-routine/

Kolb, B., & Gibb, R. (2011). Brain plasticity and behavior in the developing brain. *Journal of the Canadian Academy of Child and Adolescent Psychiatry, 20*(4), 265. https://pmc.ncbi.nlm.nih.gov/articles/PMC3222570/

LaPlante, R. (2022, June 3). *Is "sustainability" the new mindset? Part 3.* Ailuna. https://ailuna.com/sustainability-mindset-pt3/

Leader, U. (2023, May 1). *Malala Yousafzai: A tale of resilience and leadership.* Untitled Leader. https://www.untitledleader.com/lessons-in-leadership/malala-yousafzai-a-tale-of-resilience-and-leadership/

Lee, L. (2017, May 17). *Focus on small steps first, then shift to the larger goal.* Stanford Graduate School of Business. https://www.gsb.stanford.edu/insights/focus-small-steps-first-then-shift-larger-goal

Leonard, K., & Watts, R. (2024, July 9). *The ultimate guide to S.M.A.R.T. goals.* Forbes. https://www.forbes.com/advisor/business/smart-goals/

Lieder, F., Chen, P.-Z., Prentice, M., Amo, V., & Tošić, M. (2024). Gamification of behavior change: Mathematical principle and proof-of-concept study. *JMIR Serious Games, 12,* e43078. https://doi.org/10.2196/43078

Magness, J., & Magness, J. (2024, June 6). *Top 5 benefits of milestone goals: Clear direction, focus and progress.* Miviva. https://miviva.com/top-5-benefits-of-milestone-goals/

Mandino, O. (n.d.). *Og Mandino quotes.* Lifehack. https://www.lifehack.org/864437/quotes-about-setting-goals

Maricris. (2024, July 8). *Building resilience: Bouncing back from setbacks and failures.* AI Marketing Engineers. https://aimarketingengineers.com/building-resilience-bouncing-back-from-setbacks-and-failures/

Martins, J. (2024, January 23). *Strategic planning process, tips, and benefits.* Asana. https://asana.com/resources/strategic-planning

Maslach, C., & Leiter, M. P. (2016). Understanding the burnout experience: Recent research and its implications for psychiatry. *World Psychiatry, 15*(2), 103–111. https://doi.org/10.1002/wps.20311

Mckeown, G. (2014). *Essentialism: the disciplined pursuit of less.* Virgin Books.

Mead, E. (2019, June 1). *47 goal-setting exercises, tools, & games.* Positive Psychology. https://positivepsychology.com/goal-setting-exercises/

The minimalists... (n.d.). The Minimalists; The Minimalists. https://www.theminimalists.com/podcast/

My starbucks idea: An open innovation case-study. (n.d.). RGI by Ideanote. https://www.reallygoodinnovation.com/stories/my-starbucks-idea-an-open-innovation-case-study

Nolan, K. (2020, November 29). *How to plan a productive week and schedule.* Kelly Nolan | Time Management for Women. https://kellynolan.com/how-to-plan-a-productive-week-and-schedule/

Panoff, L. (2024, November 14). *11 ways to spot a fad diet (And why a balanced diet is healthier).* Verywellhealth. https://www.verywellhealth.com/fad-diets-8734078

Poor, W. (2023). Lisa's final act: How Apple invented its future by burying its past. In *The Verge.* https://www.theverge.com/23724804/lisa-computer-apple-steve-jobs-burial-utah-sun-remarketing-documentary

Primeau, M. (2021, September 15). *Your powerful, changeable mindset | Stanford Report.* News.stanford.edu. https://news.stanford.edu/stories/2021/09/mindsets-clearing-lens-life

Ratson, M. (2024, November 14). Harnessing the power of emotional transformation. *Psychology Today*. https://www.psychologytoday.com/intl/blog/the-wisdom-of-anger/202411/harnessing-the-power-of-emotional-transformation

Robinns, T. (n.d.). Tony Robbins quotes. *TagVault.org*. https://tagvault.org/blog/habits-quotes/

The role of mentorship in personal development. (n.d.). BookBaker. https://www.bookbaker.com/en/v/Growing-Up-in-Gods-Plan-The-Role-of-Mentorship-in-Personal-Development/8ae02fe2-0a23-4638-8649-242901601c4c/23

Rollyn. (2024, November 6). How to change your mindset for personal growth and success? *Serchen*. https://blog.serchen.com/how-to-change-your-mindset/

The science of well-being. (2018, March 20). Yale Online. https://online.yale.edu/courses/science-well-being

Setting personal goals. (n.d.). BookBaker. https://www.bookbaker.com/en/v/Mastering-Self-Improvement-A-Comprehensive-Guide-to-Career-Coaching-and-Guidance-Setting-Personal-Goals/8a48025e-9eb2-43b4-9d7c-fee15edf3b3b/3

Sharma, R. S. (2019). *The 5 am club : own your morning, elevate your life*. Harpercollins Publishers Ltd.

Shi, A. (2018, September 8). *Batterygate: A complete history of Apple throttling iPhones*. IFixit. https://www.ifixit.com/News/11208/batterygate-timeline

Should your exercise goals be in minutes or steps? Study suggests they are equally beneficial. (2024). ScienceDaily. https://www.sciencedaily.com/releases/2024/05/240520122655.htm

Strobl, P. (2023, November 6). *The micro-habit revolution: Transforming growth one step at a time*. Paul Strobl - Master Life Coach - Houston,

TX. https://confidecoaching.com/the-micro-habit-revolution-transforming-growth-one-step-at-a-time/

Study shows how our brains remain active during familiar, repetitive tasks | University of Cambridge. (2017). Cam.ac.uk. https://www.cam.ac.uk/research/news/study-shows-how-our-brains-remain-active-during-familiar-repetitive-tasks

Thalia. (2021, March 16). *How to build a nourishing morning and evening routine that works for you.* Notes by Thalia; Notes By Thalia. https://notesbythalia.com/morning-and-evening-routine/

Triggers. (2023, January 3). Learning Loop. https://learningloop.io/plays/psychology/triggers

Tutt, P. (2022, March 25). *6 activities that inspire a goal-setting mindset in students.* Edutopia. https://www.edutopia.org/article/6-activities-inspire-goal-setting-mindset-students/

Twenty short-term goals to improve your personal and professional life. (n.d.). *Infinity.* https://startinfinity.com/blog/short-term-goals

Unmasking self-sabotage: Are you holding yourself back? (2024, September 2). VSMG. https://vsmg.org/wellness/unmasking-self-sabotage-are-you-holding-yourself-back/

Walsch, K. (n.d.). *Kerri Walsch quotes.* A-Z Quotes. https://www.azquotes.com/quotes/topics/support-systems.html

Ward, M. (2017, January 29). *5 things you didn't know about Oprah Winfrey.* Vogue. https://www.vogue.com/article/oprah-winfrey-5-things-you-didnt-know

Westberg, P. (2024, April 9). *Inside Netflix: Innovation, originals, and cultural phenomena.* Quartr. https://quartr.com/insights/company-research/inside-netflix-innovation-originals-and-cultural-phenomena

What is your morning routine? (n.d.). My Morning Routine. https://mymorningroutine.com/qa/routine-summary/